JAPANESE
CORPORATE
PHILANTHROPY

JAPANESE
CORPORATE
PHILANTHROPY

Nancy R. London

New York   Oxford
OXFORD UNIVERSITY PRESS
1991

Oxford University Press

Oxford   New York   Toronto
Delhi   Bombay   Calcutta   Madras   Karachi
Petaling Jaya   Singapore   Hong Kong   Tokyo
Nairobi   Dar es Salaam   Cape Town
Melbourne   Auckland

and associated companies in
Berlin   Ibadan

Copyright © 1991 by Oxford University Press, Inc.

Published by Oxford University Press, Inc.,
200 Madison Avenue, New York, New York 10016

Oxford is a registered trademark of Oxford University Press

Library of Congress Cataloging-in-Publication Data
London, Nancy R.
Japanese corporate philanthropy / Nancy R. London.
p.   cm.
ISBN 0-19-506424-0
1. Corporations—Charitable contributions—Law and legislation—
Japan.   2. Charitable uses, trusts, and foundations—Japan.
3. Corporations—Charitable contributions—Social aspects—Japan.
I. Title.
LAW <JPN 7 Lond 1991>
346.52′064—dc20
[345.20664]   90-7165   CIP

2 4 6 8 9 7 5 3 1

Printed in the United States of America
on acid-free paper

*For my parents, my husband,
and the newest member
of our clan, Danielle Grace*

Preface

This book is a study of corporate philanthropy in Japan. It is a direct result of the publicity, interest, and enthusiasm generated by the spate of large Japanese corporate gifts to United States institutions – particularly to universities – that began in the early 1970s, and that are represented in the 1990s by continuing gifts to a (wider) variety of institutions and by the establishment in the United States of domestic foundations set up with Japanese corporate funds.

Appropriately, this book is also the product of cooperation and foresight on both sides of the Pacific. Large corporate grant making is in its infancy in Japan, and both the Japan Center for International Exchange in Tokyo and the Ford Foundation in New York (co-sponsors of this study) are exploring ways to encourage the expansion of philanthropic endeavors already underway and to assist the development of new, creative forms and directions in the rising "third sector" in Japan. That process is hampered at present by a lack of understanding, both within and without Japan, of the nature of Japanese philanthropy and of the cultural, legal, and procedural features that give it shape. This study was undertaken in order to help eliminate that lack, and it is to be hoped that it will succeed in some measure.

Tokyo   N.R.L.
April 1990

Acknowledgments

My sincere and overdue thanks to Susan Berresford and Paul Balaran for the idea, the support, their enthusiasm; Tadashi Yamamoto for his indispensable insights, introductions, and guidance; Michio Itō for his friendship and dedication; and to all who contributed generously of their time and endured my endless questions.

Acknowledgments

Contents

JAPANESE CORPORATE PHILANTHROPY

1

Introduction

Japanese corporate philanthropy is predominantly a phenomenon of the postwar era and, in particular, of the period of rapid reindustrialization of the country that became evident in the mid-1960s. Large-scale international corporate philanthropy — of the type that has grabbed headlines in the United States and Europe — is even newer, having begun with the Mitsubishi Group's $1 million gift to Harvard Law School in 1972 and been followed in rapid and dramatic succession by the Sumitomo Group's contribution of $2 million to Yale University in 1973 and the Mitsui Group's donation of $1 million to the Massachusetts Institute of Technology in 1974.

Although this type of international grant making is both newsworthy and commendable, it is not necessarily representative of philanthropy as practiced inside Japan. In fact, in my view, it is quite distinct from the domestic philanthropic process and has derived from a different set of goals and cultural norms.

Unlike domestic philanthropy, international grant making by Japanese companies is largely a response to external factors, both political and economic. On the political side, such grant making is part of Japan's effort to "internationalize" and to accede to the demands of other nations that Japan begin to shoulder a responsibility for international well-being commensurate with its economic strength. It stems from the same pressures that have led Japan in the past few years to increase dramatically its Overseas Development Assistance (ODA), so that today Japan's budget is on a par with that of the United States,[1] and to expand its roles in such international development organizations as the Asian Development Bank.

In particular, much of Japan's international largesse has been a direct response to political and trade pressures, especially with respect to the United States. Perhaps the most obvious example is that of the Hitachi Foundation, one of the earliest foundations to be established by a Japanese company in the United States. Established in 1985, the Hitachi Foundation was widely viewed at the time as a direct attempt to counter the negative publicity that the company generated when it was accused and successfully prosecuted in 1983 for conspiring to transport IBM's trade secrets to Japan. Similarly, after former Prime Minister Yasuhiro Nakasone's derogatory remarks in 1986 about American blacks and Hispanics, Japanese foundations and companies began donating to the United Negro College Fund, the National Association for the Advancement of Colored People, the Congress of Racial Equality, and other similar groups.

On the economic side, "good corporate citizenship" is good business. It is, therefore, no coincidence that the growth of international corporate philanthropy has paralleled the tremendous growth of Japanese international corporate business.[2] As Japanese companies have expanded their presence in the United States, they have realized that American society expects a lot from big business — particularly in the form of time and money donated to charity — and they have set out to fulfill some of those expectations.

In the nonprofit as well as the for-profit world, Japan has proved masterful in adapting to and adopting foreign practices that it admires or that may be economically beneficial. The blockbuster gifts to U.S. museums and universities, far from being typically Japanese are, rather, export products carefully tailored like many others to suit overseas markets. These grants are of a magnitude unknown in Japan where, for the most part, philanthropy is conducted in a more organic, less obvious, and less ostentatious manner.

For example, in the spring of 1989, Matsushita Electric Company of America, following a suggestion made by the president of Minolta Corporation at a Japan Society meeting in New York, committed to contributing 0.1 percent of its annual U.S. sales revenues to U.S. nonprofit organizations. With an estimated $4 billion projected for 1989 sales, this meant for Matsushita Electric a 1989 contributions budget of $4 million, approximately three times the company's then current contributions budget. Not only am I unaware of this kind of percentage test being used by any individual company in Japan as a means of establishing giving targets, but I am also unaware of any company in Japan consciously publicizing its domestic giving in such an open manner.[3] Even more significantly, the pure size of the contribution is on a scale that would be exceptional by domestic standards.[4]

Partly as a result of the less ostentatious giving style prevalent in Japan, no statistics are readily available for the magnitude of domestic corporate giving on a company-by-company basis. If we use corporate foundation giving as a rough indication, however, it is clear that grants of this size within Japan are unusual. The majority of grant-making foundations in Japan have an annual contributions budget of approximately ¥25 million, or $179,000 (at an exchange rate of ¥140/$1). Only 1.8 percent (which represents only approximately eighteen foundations) have budgets exceeding ¥500 million, or $3.6 million.[5] By contrast, in 1988, Hitachi Chemical, in the largest single Japanese grant to date to the United States, gave $12 million to the University of California at Irvine to support biotechnology research.

Even more important and more striking than the differences in grant-making style between Japanese companies in Japan and Japanese companies overseas is that the private nonprofit sector as a whole is still relatively unknown and underutilized in Japan.[6] Most Japanese are not familiar with the concept of nonprofit organizations, much less with their activities. "What is a nonprofit organization, and why are you interested in it?" was the question I most frequently encountered when discussing my research with Japanese who were not themselves involved in nonprofit activities.

The reasons for stressing the divergence in style between international and domestic grant making and for emphasizing the relative unimportance of the private nonprofit "third sector" in Japan are several: First, my purpose most assuredly is not to criticize; rather, it is to describe Japanese corporate philanthropy in a way that makes it comprehensible, especially to non-Japanese. The highly publicized international grant making since the early to mid-1970s is only one aspect of Japanese philanthropy, and not its most representative aspect. Nonetheless, because of the attention focused on those gifts, many outside Japan have developed inflated and/or inaccurate expectations of what Japanese philanthropy is.

Because Japanese giving in the United States has been carried out at least superficially in the "American style," or in what is perceived as the American style, there has been a tendency to assume that

Japanese philanthropy in general duplicates the American style. But it does not and, I believe, is not likely to do so in the near future, with the possible exception of certain kinds of international grants. Thinking otherwise can lead to tensions in this area as surely as misunderstanding has led to tensions in the realm of politics, trade, and commerce.

I am aware of one case already in which a major U.S. institution succeeded in raising substantial funds in Japan and then, due to simple misunderstanding and miscommunication, disappointed the unspoken expectations of their Japanese donors that the grant would be widely and lavishly publicized in the United States. As a result, the Japanese woman who spearheaded the fund-raising effort reported, "I have been personally embarrassed and cannot hope to approach these sources for funding on behalf of [this institution] or any other for a long, long time."[7]

For their part, many Japanese, too, have misunderstood and misapplied some elements of the American philanthropic tradition. In their zeal to adapt and to be perceived as "classy corporations, not just selling machines,"[8] they have sometimes gone overboard, and their grant making has backfired, creating tensions where it was intended to have alleviated them and eliciting reactions like the following from Chalmers Johnson, professor of international relations at the University of California at San Diego: "Some Japanese support for research is predatory. . . . It is to buy research they can't get otherwise."[9]

The second reason for stressing the differences between Japanese and U.S. philanthropy is that increasingly during my five years of living in Japan, I encountered American organizations trying to raise funds in Japan, interested in joint-venture projects with their Japanese counterparts, or endeavoring to establish nonprofit organizations in Japan.[10] For any of these projects to be fruitful, an awareness of and a familiarity with the concerns, legal forms, and processes that dominate Japanese domestic philanthropy are critical.

Foreign organizations and their representatives who come to Japan expecting to find the philanthropic process similar to that at home are often daunted and disappointed by their lack of success or by the amount of effort required to achieve even a small success, especially in fundraising. One American university representative, seeking funds to establish a campus in Japan, bemoaned the months he had spent soliciting a particular donor that ultimately offered a $2 million contribution but then asked in exchange for access to one of the university's large research facilities. "The proffered grant was not even close to being of a magnitude that would persuade us to consider such an offer."[11] As a result of this and similar experiences, many have complained about what they perceive as a lack of philanthropic spirit in Japan.

Professor Yujiro Hayashi, former executive director of the Toyota Foundation, believes that one sign of maturity in a society is the degree to which the third sector is firmly established and that because the nonprofit sector is not firmly established in Japan, Japan has an "immature social infrastructure."[12] This is not the same as saying, however, that the Japanese lack a philanthropic or charitable spirit. Commenting on the difficulties of fund-raising in Japan relative to other wealthy nations, Mr. David Exley, former director of UNICEF in Japan, observed, "There's been a lot of catching up. . . . But Japan has a long way to go and a lot more catching up to do. . . . In terms of personal generosity, Japanese are second to none. But sometimes when it gets beyond that to 'we really must do something to help' they don't really relate it to themselves."[13]

This brings me to the third reason for stressing the differences between Japanese and U.S. philanthropy. Japanese philanthropy (even that outside Japan) functions in a uniquely Japanese social, historical, and cultural context. As society evolves, so will philanthropy, but it still must be viewed in its own context to be properly understood. Toward that end, the next chapter will identify certain elements of the sociocultural framework that seem to have had, and continue to have, considerable impact on the development and pursuit of nonprofit activities in Japan. These elements will recur, more and less obviously, and should be kept in mind throughout the remainder of this book.

Finally, there is a more mundane and practical reason for stressing the differences between the third sector in Japan and that in the United States, namely, that because of its fledgling state and status, Japanese philanthropy has not been widely studied even in Japan. As a journalist friend observed: "The Japanese are notorious for collecting data. If they haven't done it with respect to philanthropy, the subject can't be very important." That has begun to change, however, and more and more articles, papers, and seminars are being devoted to the topic. Nonetheless, at present, both factual and analytic materials on the subject are scarce. Where such materials do exist, I have used them. My research, however, was predominantly a series of interviews with foundations, corporations, government officials, fund givers, and fund seekers. The result is a compilation of impressions, anecdotes, and opinions, both mine and those of the many people who were kind enough to answer my lengthy and no doubt frequently baffling questions.

Notes

1. In 1988, Japan's ODA totaled $9.1 billion on a net disbursement basis, whereas the United States' ODA totaled $9.8 billion. Hideharu Torii, "Subsidy for Private Aid Units Raises Hope of Effectiveness, Fear of Control," *Japan Times*, September 5, 1989, p. 3.

2. Not surprisingly, the mounting Japanese direct investment in Asia over the past several years has increased the amount of corporate philanthropic activity in the region. Thus, although the United States still receives the major part of Japanese international philanthropic giving, Asia is consuming an ever-growing percentage. See Chapter 7.

3. As detailed further in Chapter 6, to determine the contributions targets of its member companies, the Keidanren often uses a percentage test of one kind or another, such as percentage of sales or percentage of production. However, the relevant percentages, and even the fact of their use, are rather closely guarded — certainly never publicized — by the Keidanren.

The notion of using such a percentage basis, as proposed by Minolta and adopted by Matsushita, may derive either from this practice by the Keidanren or from the percentage-giving goals established by certain U.S. companies. In the latter case, the relevant measure is usually 1 or 2 percent of "pretax income" rather than a percentage of sales.

4. It is interesting that Matsushita Electric, which not only has committed to such generous direct funding but also has established a foundation in the United States with assets of about $11 million, is the largest single Japanese employer in the United States, with over eight thousand employees.

5. Tadashi Yamamoto and Takayoshi Amenomori, "Japanese Private Philanthropy in an Interdependent World" (paper prepared for Organized Private Philanthropy in East and Southeast Asia, a seminar held in Bang-

kok, Thailand, August 7-10, 1989), relying on statistics compiled by the Foundation Library Center of Japan.

6. In recent years, several organizations have made concerted efforts to raise the public's awareness of and familiarity with nonprofit activities, both corporate and noncorporate. These organizations include the Japan Center for International Exchange, the Japan Association of Charitable Corporations, the Sasakawa Peace Foundation, the Foundation Library of Japan, and the Japanese NGO (nongovernmental organization) Center for International Cooperation.

7. Interview with Mrs. Hanako Matano, July 18, 1986.

8. Mr. Norio Hira, president of Hakuhodo Advertising America, as quoted in "Japan Digs Deep to Win the Hearts and Minds of America," *Business Week*, July 11, 1988, p. 39.

9. Ibid., quoting Professor Chalmers Johnson.

10. In the latter category, those endeavoring to establish nonprofit organizations in Japan were U.S. companies doing business in Japan and seeking to be good corporate citizens, by either setting up company-giving programs or forming foundations. In most cases, direct-giving programs have been preferred because of the bureaucratic difficulties of setting up a foundation. U.S. universities, many of which have been actively courted by the Japanese to set up overseas campuses, have also been actively exploring the nonprofit system. Finally, there is some indication that a variety of U.S.-based nonprofit organizations (universities being the most prevalent) are now beginning to do what the Japanese have done in reverse for years, namely, to open local representative offices to coordinate fund-raising activities.

11. Details of the interview withheld at the request of the interviewee.

12. Yujiro Hayashi, "Before the Dawn, an Immature Social Infrastructure," Executive Director's Report, The Toyota Foundation Annual Report, fiscal 1977, Tokyo.

13. Maggie Jackson, "Charities Go Begging in Well-Off Japan," AP Wire Service, September 10, 1987.

2

Themes and Corollaries

At a Japan Society meeting in 1985, Mr. Den Fujita, the maverick president of McDonald's Japan, was asked why Japan did not participate more actively and more generously in philanthropic activities either domestically or internationally. Mr. Fujita's response was simple: "Because we are not Christian." In fact, his response was too simple.

Many people, like Mr. Fujita, have cited religion as the major factor militating against the growth of private philanthropy in Japan. Although it is certainly a factor, it is not the only factor. Rather, religion is an integral part of the complex of features that mold the Japanese character and hence the Japanese attitude toward philanthropy.

Definition of Society and Social Obligation

The Position of the Individual in Society

One way in which religious influence—notably Buddhist influence—manifests itself in Japan is in the lack of centrality of the individual. According to Tokyo University Professor Hajime Nakamura:

> The followers of Pure Land Buddhism, instead of saying "I will do this or that," often say "I will have you allow me to do this or that." This kind of phrasing, moreover, is frequently used by Japanese in general. . . . The recognition implied by saying "I will have you allow me to do this" is that the individual, as a limited entity, could not do such and such unaided. Only with the help of all others concerned and trusting to the grace of heaven and earth can the individual gain a position in which he or she can do this or that.[1]

According to anthropologists and sociologists, this aspect of Buddhism is itself characteristic of *high-context*, or high-density, populations (Japan being a high-context culture and the United States being a *low-context* culture), in which there is not much demarcation between the ego and others. Thus the greatest sin in this kind of group- and consensus-oriented society is unilateral action.[2]

Because the Buddhist view is that individuals acting alone can accomplish nothing, individuals tend to organize themselves, define their identities, and make decisions in terms of groups. How, then, is group defined? In the opinion of several prominent scholars, the definition is a functional one based on the old clan system of shared property and "pseudoconsanguineous" relationships, rather than on actual blood ties or other abstract notions such as mercurial exchange or community.[3] In any event, the group is held together by a series of functional relationships, and the most obvious manifestation of such functional relationships today is the company or groups of companies.

According to biblical scholar and publisher, Mr. Shichihei Yamamoto, these functional groups, of which the company is the most prominent example, define the community to which individuals feel responsible: "While villagers in Britain leave their communities each morning and commute to work, the reverse is the case in Japan. Here one is always a part of the company community, and the neighborhood is merely the place one happens to sleep. . . . Japanese will gladly work overtime for nothing, yet they are loath to do anything for their neighborhood."[4]

Professor Hayashi, too, believes that although Japanese are accustomed to identifying themselves as members of groups composed of individuals, they are not accustomed to seeing themselves as members of a mass of undifferentiated individuals. The Western concept of society refers to just such an undifferentiated mass. In support of his contention, Mr. Hayashi pointed out that until Meiji times (1868–1912) the Japanese language did not have a word for *society*. The one that has been used since exposure to the Western concept — *shakai* — is not, according to Hayashi, in all respects congruous with what Westerners see as society: "Our comprehension of society as a collection of many and unspecified persons is still weak."[5]

The consequences for philanthropy of the Japanese view of the individual and the individual's relationship to society are numerous. Perhaps foremost is the fact that Japanese define the community to which they are responsible and to which they owe a philanthropic obligation differently from the way that most Westerners do. The relevant community is not the undifferentiated mass of society but, rather, that contained group of people with whom one has some relationship. These people are *uchi* (inside), and all others are *soto* (outside). Obligations generally do not extend outside.

In this context, it is interesting to note that just as there was no equivalent in the Japanese language for the term *society* until the Meiji era, there really is no equivalent in Japanese today for the word *philanthropy*. In discussions of eleemosynary issues in Japan, the English word *philanthropy* (now incorporated into Japanese) is used. The literal meaning of philanthropy is "love of mankind," from the Greek *phil* plus *anthropos*, an encompassing, abstract concept that has little to do with the traditional Japanese view of tangible, functional ties between individuals or groups of individuals. This point was brought home to me one day in a conversation with a Japanese friend who observed that most Japanese routinely and voluntarily contribute money to defray the funeral costs of a member of a friend's or colleague's family but that these same people would be nonplussed to be asked to contribute to a funeral society for the benefit of the general public.

Related to the question of "to whom is charity due?" is the issue of "by whom should charity be performed?" That question has traditionally been answered differently in Japan, as evidenced by the fact that philanthropy by individuals in Japan is extremely rare. Accordingly, this book is about corporate philanthropy because philanthropy in Japan is essentially corporate. There are corporate foundations and corporate-giving programs run directly by companies, but large-scale individual philanthropy and independent foundations are virtually unknown, particularly in comparison with the United States, where the overwhelming majority of charitable contributions in any year are made by individuals.[6] Other than contributions to religious organizations, temples, and shrines, individuals in Japan give very little in either time or money to nonprofit organizations.

There are, of course, noteworthy exceptions, and times are changing because of greater wealth, increasingly diverse social demands, heightened social and international awareness, and more exposure to the West.[7] Nonetheless, there is no tradition as such of individual giving, premised on the assumption that the individual has an obligation (religious or otherwise) and the ability to contribute to society through unilateral action. According to Mr. Yoshifumi Matsuda, a senior official at the Ministry of Foreign Affairs, "The concept of private citizens working for the public cause is something new to us."[8]

Moreover, in the traditional Japanese view, any action that focuses attention on the individual and differentiates that individual from the group is to be frowned on, as illustrated by the famous Japanese saying "the nail that sticks up gets hammered down." Thus, it is not that philanthropy by individuals is inappropriate but, rather, that philanthropy by individuals is not as appropriate as is philanthropy by the undifferentiated group or corporation.

The paucity of philanthropy by individuals is reflected in and, some would argue, perpetuated by the structure of the tax law. As I shall discuss in more detail later, individuals receive almost no tax deduction for either lifetime gifts or bequests to charity, whereas corporations can deduct their contributions to a wide variety of nonprofit entities.

The lack of an individual philanthropic tradition necessarily colors and influences the role that corporate philanthropists define for themselves in Japanese society, just as the existence of a longstanding tradition of individual giving in the United States has influenced the course and philosophy of U.S. corporate philanthropy.

In the early years of corporate philanthropy in the United States, people struggled (and still do) to define an appropriate justification and role for corporate giving by reference to the individual tradition. Although the charitable deduction for corporations existed in the Internal Revenue Code as early as 1936, that provision was not widely used by companies nor was the concept of corporate contributions generally accepted until sometime later by shareholders as an appropriate use of corporate profits.

In a landmark case decided by the New Jersey Supreme Court in 1953, a stockholder sued the A. P. Smith Manufacturing Company for damages resulting from the company's "improper" use of corporate funds to make a $1,500 contribution to Princeton University. The unanimous opinion of the court, however, recognized the concept and importance of good corporate citizenship as extending beyond the mere production of profits, stating:

> When the wealth of the nation was primarily in the hands of individuals, they discharged their responsibilities as citizens by donating freely for charitable purposes. With the transfer of wealth to corporate hands and the imposition of heavy burdens of individual taxation, they have been unable to keep pace with increased philanthropic needs. They have therefore, with justification, turned to corporations to assume the modern obligations of good citizenship in the same manner as humans do.[9]

In this case, and in its resolution, are the seeds of the tension that still exists in defining the role of corporate philanthropy in the United States. From the point of view of the corporate shareholder, the expenditure of company profits that otherwise might be distributed in the form of dividends must be justified from a business perspective. In other words, corporate "good citizenship" has to have some kind of direct or indirect monetary or public relations benefit for the company, no matter how attenuated. Too much benefit to the company, however, can lead others to feel that the contribution is not altruistic enough, is not really philanthropy — or not philanthropy as they know it.[10]

Although corporate philanthropy in Japan can be as public relations and market oriented as it is anywhere else — Waldemar Nielson called it "primitive" in this regard — at least some of the soul-searching, agonizing, and perhaps even dissembling involved in the search for a justifiable motive in the United States has been avoided in Japan. Corporate philanthropy is what it is — a mixture of altruistic and economic motivations, with the balance of the mixture depending on the particular corporation and the specific grant — and is accepted as such.[11]

Some Japanese feel that the lack of a separate, independent philanthropic tradition in Japan has made it difficult for Japanese companies to see their giving activities as anything other than purely self-serving; others feel that it actually has enabled some Japanese corporate philanthropists to be more independent and less market oriented than are corporate philanthropists elsewhere. According to Mr. Hideo Yamaguchi of the Toyota Foundation, corporate foundations in Japan often play the dual role that independent foundations and corporate foundations jointly play in the United States: "Because Japan does not have independent foundations, sometimes corporate foundations have to behave better than American corporate foundations."[12] Mr. Tom Fox, of the Council on Foundations (U.S.), similarly feels that Japanese corporate foundations often seem more independent—or at least are structured to give that appearance—than do their U.S. counterparts.[13]

Even among corporations, the disinclination to stand out and to be an "individual" influences patterns of philanthropy. Significantly, like individuals, companies in Japan have traditionally preferred to contribute to philanthropic causes as a group. As Chapter 6 explains in more detail, it is often industrial and business associations that handle fund-raising and grant-making requests on behalf of their member companies. These associations (for which the umbrella association is the Keidanren) usually follow a formulaic approach in determining what percentage of any particular grant request a given company should bear.

The advantage of this system is that each company knows what is expected of it and, equally importantly, what is expected of its competitors and compatriots. The risk of embarrassment through contributing too little or too much is thus eliminated. According to Mr. Hachiro Koyama, founder of the Japan Fulbright Foundation, "The Japanese like balance. If they give too much they create envy, if they give too little they lose face, and so they prefer to have someone else decide what is appropriate."[14]

On *and* giri — *Obligation and Gratitude*

Consistent with the differing Japanese and Western definitions of society and the individual's role in society is a divergent view of what motivates people to contribute to their society in the form of philanthropy. This also has ties to religion. It is commonly believed that philanthropy in the West was originally a means of giving evidence of atonement for sin, original or otherwise, and of serving God by serving society as a whole. By contrast, in Japan, the motivation seems to be not so much a desire to expunge sin by serving society as a whole (because, as we noted, there is not a well-established definition of society in Japan, and in any event the perception of what an individual can do is limited) but, rather, a duty to repay *on*, or debts of obligation, and to express *giri*, or gratitude owed to various groups or sectors of society.

It is therefore no coincidence that the earliest Japanese foundations, including those active before World War II, tended to incorporate the word *on* into their names.[15] These foundations provided a means for companies to fulfill an obligation, to repay a debt of gratitude to a society that fostered their growth and helped them achieve their economic goals. Even today, foundations are often formed or major grants are given on an anniversary of a company's founding, and it is quite common to read in the statement by the company or foundation president sentiments expressing gratitude to a nurturing society and/or to devoted employees.[16]

On can exist among individuals or groups or between an individual and a group, but regardless of its form, it presupposes some kind of relationship, that is, a functional relationship of the type referred to by Mr. Shichihei Yamamoto earlier in this chapter. Obligation and gratitude cannot exist between people or entities that have never before encountered each other; accordingly, it is difficult for philanthropy to occur between entities that have not previously encountered each other in some way. As Mr. Mikio Kato of the International House of Japan observed, "In Japan we do not give to the anonymous crowd or to anonymous causes. Mail solicitation of contributions such as is common in the United States is virtually unknown and really would be anathema here. But people will gladly give to friends or to fellow employees, for any reason."[17]

To the extent that the award of a grant is seen as a repayment of a debt or an expression of gratitude, the objective merits of a particular grant proposal may take on a secondary importance. Certainly this is not always the case, but one Japanese philanthropist feels that the "gratitude" element colors the Japanese view of grant making and distinguishes it from that in the United States. "Because grants are often made out of gratitude or friendship, it is not the custom to inquire too deeply into exactly how money will be used and for what purpose. The grant is seen as a gift or a repayment, not an investment. This makes grant supervision and oversight seem unnecessary."[18]

This view of grant making also accounts, to some extent, for the dilemma faced by many Japanese corporations and business associations when they are approached by foreign organizations (as they have been more and more in recent years) for funding. They are not so much unwilling to respond as they are stymied by requests from organizations with which they have no prior relationship and of which they often have no prior knowledge. Lacking the skill and knowledge to assess grant proposals on their merits and lacking, at the same time, a clear sense of the soliciting organization, they are at a loss to understand why the organization has approached them and how or why they should respond. Just as in the Japanese language itself it is necessary to know the status of the person to whom one is speaking before one can choose the appropriate level of linguistic deference or condescension,[19] so for a potential granter it is necessary to understand the status of the grantee in relation to itself before an appropriate reply can be crafted.

On the other side, the pervasiveness of *on* and *giri* contribute to the aforementioned stylistic differences between corporate grant making inside and outside Japan and help explain what some American fund-raisers have found to be a disconcertingly aggressive, "what-do-we-get-in-return-for-our-contribution" approach. As an initial matter, and almost by definition, foreigners and foreign organizations are *soto*: outside a Japanese context and outside the ties of *on* and *giri*. Lacking confidence that foreigners will understand and/or honor these complex relationships, Japanese may tend to be more aggressive in their international grant making than they would be at home, both in how they contribute and what they request in return. By contrast, in a domestic context, not only is the quid pro quo implicitly understood, but there also is less urgency about its immediate and direct fulfillment. It is understood that relationships will endure over a long period and that over the course of such relationships, repayment may be accomplished by a variety of means and with varying degrees of subtlety.

The Role of Law in Society

Because of the predominance of personal relationships in defining and cementing functional groups, and the role of interlocking obligation and gratitude debts in structuring those relationships, the necessity for law and legal relationships in Japan is diminished. Law and contract define relationships in societies in which people lack other, more organic forms of cohesion. But such is not the case in Japan. According to Mr. Shichihei Yamamoto, "There is one vitally important sociological concept that applies to every country but Japan. It is the concept of religion and norms based on contracts." (Japanese understand contracts and honor them, but society runs on consensus, not contract) . . . "consensus means more than law to them."[20]

Although it is debatable whether Japan is in fact the only society for which this is true, there is no question but that law and contract are more flexible notions in Japan than they are in the West. "In Japan a contract might be said to contain only one provision of overriding importance: that in the event of disagreement both parties will discuss the matter in good faith. If a contract is concluded at all, it is no more than a document affirming the tradition of dialogue."[21] This view of law as providing a basis for dialogue, and of contract as representing the end product of dialogue, is nowhere more apparent than in the laws and procedures governing nonprofit organizations and philanthropic activities generally.

As I shall describe more fully in subsequent chapters, the actual law concerned with philanthropy in Japan is scant and sketchy. This skeletal structure is supplemented by largely informal "administrative guidance" issued by various ministries of the government, but what truly structures the nonprofit sector is a process of dialogue, negotiation, compromise, and consensus, following generally the outlines provided by law.[22] For better and for worse, this system is flexible, often arbitrary, responsive to, and molded by the strength of personal relationships, influential contacts, and burdens of *on* and *giri*. As with many areas of Japanese law, the fluidity of the system makes generalization and predictability extremely difficult. This in turn is frustrating to Americans and other foreigners who want to understand exactly how the system works and is equally frustrating to many in Japan who are trying to work within the system.

Attitude Toward Government — *okami*

One manifestation of the differing Japanese and Western attitudes toward the role of the individual and individual initiative in society is the deference given in Japan to the government and the government's wisdom in making choices and providing services on behalf

11. Of course, it is also likely that there is less soul-searching because the topic as a whole does not merit much attention in Japan; accordingly, people have not focused on defining an appropriate role for corporate philanthropy. Those who do concern themselves with the issue have for the most part accepted the view popular in the United States of "enlightened self-interest" as the impetus and justification for corporate philanthropy.

12. Interview with Mr. Hideo Yamaguchi, April 28, 1987.

13. Discussions with Mr. Tom Fox, October 16, 1986.

14. Sometimes giving within an industrial association is anonymous and sometimes participants are known, but either way, the donor has the security of having done what was appropriate in the eyes of the group.

15. Among the earliest foundations were Kan'onko (meaning, roughly, "Society of gratitude") established in 1827; Saito hō'onkai (Hō'onkai translates as "Society for repaying gratitude"), established in 1923; and Mitsui hō-onkai, established in 1934.

16. Approximately 70 percent of the foundations that I interviewed for this book were established on the occasion of an anniversary of the company's founding.

17. Interview with Mr. Mikio Kato, associate managing director, International House of Japan, March 16, 1987.

18. Details of interview withheld at the request of the interviewee.

19. In the Japanese language, pronouns, adjectives, and verb conjugation vary according to the sex and status of the person being spoken to or spoken about, in relation to oneself.

20. Yamamoto, "Consanguineous and Territorial Societies," p. 1, quoting political scientist Naoki Komuro; and Yamamoto, "Contract Versus Consensus," p. 1.

21. Yamamoto, "Contract Versus Consensus," p. 1.

22. Although such administrative guidance often has the force of law, it is not issued through formal, legally dictated channels. There is, in fact, very little statutory authority for issuing such guidance.

23. Yujiro Hayashi, "The Role of Private Philanthropy in Japan," in *The Role of Philanthropy in International Cooperation*, Report on the JCIE 15th Anniversary, International Symposium (Tokyo: Japan Center for International Exchange, December 1985), p. 5.

24. Interview with Mr. Mikio Kato, March 16, 1987. Mr. Kato cited the Japan Foundation (see the discussion of the Japan Foundation in Chapter 5) as a prime casualty of this circular logic. Initially, the Japan Foundation, established at the initiative of the Foreign Ministry, was to have received half of its funding from the government and half from the private sector, but once the government had funded its half, the private sector withdrew. To this day, the foundation has received very little funding from private

of its people. The government in Japan is referred to, only semi-facetiously, as *okami*, or god ("kami" preceded by an honorific).

The difference, in particular, between Japanese and American attitudes toward government is often cited by Japanese as a major reason for the divergent development of philanthropy in the two countries. As Mr. Yujiro Hayashi pointed out, "the Japanese tend to forget that laws and government are of their own creation and expect public bodies to take responsibility for various aspects of society. Americans, on the other hand, ever since their nation's founding, have felt the need to make up for the deficiencies of the government, with private philanthropy being one outgrowth of this outlook."[23]

The United States is unique in its reliance on the private, nonprofit sector to provide necessary social and cultural services. In contrast with many Americans, most Japanese expect and prefer to have government provide for them. The government, too, prefers it that way. One could debate *ad infinitum* which system is "better," and the chances are that Americans would still come out in favor of the private sector and that Japanese would still come out in favor of the government, but the ultimate issue really is "Are society's needs being met in an efficient and humane way?" It would be difficult to say that Japan's are not or that they are being met less well than any other society's needs.

Not only has traditional reliance on government obviated the need and desire for a strong private sector, but it also has created a private sector in which the government plays a large role. As detailed in Chapters 3 through 5, nonprofit organizations are incorporated, licensed, and taxed at the pleasure and subject to the discretion of various branches of the government. Many feel that nonprofit status is conferred grudgingly by the government, which takes the position that "if the activities of these organizations are important enough to merit special status under the law, they are important enough for the government to do by itself without input from the private sector." According to Mr. Mikio Kato, the government's attitude creates a rather circular problem. If the project that a nonprofit organization wants to carry out is deemed important, then the government wants a hand in it; at the same time, once the government steps in, private initiative will languish because people feel that the government is taking care of the matter and is probably best suited to do so in the long run.[24]

Japan As a Middle-Class Society

Another element impeding the growth of the third sector in Japan is the widespread disbelief among Japanese in Japan's current wealth. "Only recently have the Japanese begun . . . to accept the reality that they are not so poor as they used to believe," noted Mr. Osamu Muro, an expert on Third World nongovernmental aid.[25] Even though Japan is now reputed to have more billionaires (per capita) than the United States has and is the home of many of the world's largest companies, the Japanese persist in seeing themselves as solidly middle class and are fond of saying that Japan is a rich country full of poor people.

Undoubtedly the accumulation of large personal and industrial fortunes has contributed to the growth of Japanese philanthropy since the 1960s, much as it did in the United States at the turn of the century, but not as much as it might have if that wealth were generally acknowledged. With respect to individuals, studies conducted in the United States indicate that it is both wealthy people and people who perceive themselves as having sufficient discretionary, disposable income who are the most generous contributors to charitable causes.

A study commissioned by the Rockefeller Brothers Fund and conducted by the Independent Sector in 1986 found that at all income levels, those who believed that they had discretionary income gave more generously to charity than did those who did not. The study further found that those who reported they had little or no worry about money needs in the future were also more generous contributors.[26] Both of these observations have implications for giving in Japan where—due to the high price of land and housing and the absence of a social security system to defray the costs of retirement—most Japanese save assiduously, do not feel they have large amounts of discretionary income, and worry greatly about their financial reserves for the future.

Notes

1. Yujiro Hayashi, "Toward Japanese Philanthropy," quoted in *The Future of Private Grant-Making Foundations*, Proceedings of the Tenth-Anniversary International Symposium of the Toyota Foundation (Tokyo: Toyota Foundation, 1985), p. 62.

2. Shichihei Yamamoto, "Contract Versus Consensus," in *Entrepreneurship: The Japanese Experience*, vol. 3 (Kyoto: PHP Institute, 1982), p. 3.

3. Chie Nakane, "Organizational Comparison Between Japanese and Southeast Asians," in *In Search of Meaningful Cultural Exchange: Southeast Asia and Japan* (Tokyo: Japan Foundation, 1980), pp. 169–170; and Shichihei Yamamoto, "Consanguineous and Territorial Societies," in *Entrepreneurship: The Japanese Experience*, vol. 2 (Kyoto: PHP Institute, 1982), pp. 1–4.

4. Yamamoto, "Consanguineous and Territorial Societies," p. 7.

5. Hayashi, "Toward Japanese Philanthropy," p. 60.

6. In the United States, individual philanthropy is the base from which corporate philanthropy derives. Although corporate philanthropy in the United States has grown dramatically since it first became acceptable in the mid-1950s, 85 to 90 percent of the total dollar amount dedicated to charitable causes in most years comes from individuals, whereas only 4 to 5 percent comes from corporations.

7. In particular, individual initiatives have been noteworthy and on the rise in the realm of nongovernmental organizations (NGOs). Although the total size and number of these development organizations are still extremely small—270 NGOs in all—more than 30 percent have been established by private citizens' groups with largely or wholly private funds. See *Directory of Non-Governmental Organizations in Japan: NGO's Active in Development Cooperation* (Tokyo: Japanese NGO Center for International Cooperation [JANIC], 1988).

8. As quoted in Amy Borrus et al., "Japan Digs Deep to Win the Hearts and Minds of America," *Business Week*, July 11, 1988, p. 39.

9. *A.P. Smith Mfg. Co. v. Barlow*, 97 A. 2d 180 (Super. Ct. N.J. 1953), *affirmed*, 98 A. 2d 581 (S. Ct. N.J. 1953), *appeal dismissed*, 346 U.S. 861 (1953).

10. In this regard, it is interesting to note that until 1936, companies could deduct gifts to charities only if they qualified as business expenses. With the amendment in 1936 of what is now Section 170 of the Internal Revenue Code, companies were relieved of the burden of proving the business purpose of their gifts. For a two-year period, corporations could make contributions and deduct them as either charitable contributions or business expenses. Then in 1938, the Internal Revenue Code was once again amended, this time to deny corporations the right to deduct charitable gifts as business expenses. This was intended to emphasize (perhaps unrealistically) the "pure," altruistic motives of corporate giving, but according to Boris Bittker, it mainly serves as a reminder of the business context in which such gifts are actually made. See Boris Bittker, "Charitable Contributions: Tax Deductions or Matching Grants?" *Tax Law Review* 28 (1972), pp. 57–58.

sources, but it does receive designated donations from private business that it then channels to the specified donees.

25. Jackson, "Charities Go Begging."

26. In 1984, 34 percent of those responding to the Independent Sector survey who reported that they had moderate to large amounts of discretionary income gave an average of $1,120, compared with $510 for the 49 percent of respondents who reported that they had a small amount of discretionary income, and $250 for the 27 percent of respondents who reported that they had no discretionary income. See *The Charitable Behavior of Americans*, Findings from a National Survey (commissioned by the Rockefeller Brothers Fund) (Washington, D.C.: Independent Sector, 1986).

3

The Development of the Nonprofit System

Economic growth and prosperity in Japan have led to an increased concern with and ability to provide for social welfare. At the same time, political pressure and the growing diversity of society have begun to alter traditional perceptions of what constitutes social welfare and by what means it ought to be looked after.

Social welfare, or social activities in the public interest, is normally provided through three different channels—public institutions (i.e., the government or its agencies), private profit-making institutions (corporations), and private non-profit-making or voluntary organizations—each of which has its own means and ends. In the case of profit-making organizations, activities are conducted primarily for economic gain, but indirectly, social welfare is advanced through research, provision of products and services, and employment. In the case of both government and nonprofit organization activities, the public good is more directly advanced (targeted), but while the government's motivation is essentially political, the voluntary organization's motivation is thought to be humanitarian or charitable.

The balance among these three different mechanisms and their degree of separation from one another varies from society to society and constitutes one of the major distinctions between Japan and the United States and, in particular, between Japanese and U.S.-style philanthropy. Japan has been, remains, and will probably continue for the foreseeable future to be much more reliant on government-provided services (and on corporate-provided services) than the United States is. I alluded earlier to some of the reasons for this. In addition, as mentioned in Chapter 2, the boundary between government and other nonprofit organization activities in Japan often is not clearly delineated.

Nonprofit organizations in Japan run the gamut from wholly private to almost wholly public, that is, government sponsored, funded, and controlled. Truly private, "charitable" nonprofit organizations—those that generally correspond to the U.S. category of 501(c)(3) charitable organizations—such as the corporate foundations that are the focus of this book, are a relatively new and very small subset of the total group termed nonprofit.[1] In the minds of the public (and often in the view of the government), the distinction between private and other nonprofit organizations is not at all clear, which has created some misperceptions and negative perceptions about the nature and function of private philanthropy in Japan.

In order to place private philanthropy and private foundations in their proper historical and legal context, this chapter will briefly trace the development of the nonprofit sector as a whole and then will separate out that group of private organizations relevant to this study.

The Civil Code and *kōekihōjin*

As in Europe and the United States, the earliest nonprofit organizations in Japan were religious—Buddhist temples and Shinto shrines—which, in addition to their religious activities, offered a variety of social and educational services. There is evidence of this type of activity in Japan as early as the eighth century and continuing through the Edo period (1603–1868) in the form of fund-raising to build temples and support for private education.

Toward the end of the Edo period, in 1829, the Akita kan'on ko (*kan'on* means gratitude; see Chapter 2), regarded by most as the first organized private philanthropic organization in Japan, was established by a merchant serving a lord in the Akita domain. This organization offered help to poor farmers, sought to alleviate the financial distress of the domain, and supported orphaned children. According to historical records, approximately two hundred people in the region joined together and pooled their funds to purchase a piece of land that served as an endowment supporting the organization's activities.[2]

Despite this interesting example, the shogunate as well as the provincial lords of the Edo period were the main providers for the public welfare. Their highly centralized, tightly controlled system of government left little room for, and gave little encouragement to, the development of privately sponsored public-benefit initiatives. The more contemporary concept of nonprofit organization really began with the concerted modernization of Japan during the Meiji Restoration, beginning in 1868, and with the passage of the current Civil Code in 1898.[3]

Article 34 of the Civil Code states: "An association or foundation relating to worship, religion, charity, science, art or otherwise relating to public interests and not having for its object the acquisition of gain may be made a juristic person subject to the permission of the competent authorities." This provision, like most of the Japanese Civil Code, is closely modeled on the German Civil Code (especially the draft of 1888) and incorporates that law's reliance on administrative approval and supervision of private, nonprofit initiatives, something that did not exist in relation to the early Buddhist organizations.

The provision itself is not unique. Nonprofit organizations around the world exist at the pleasure of the relevant governing authorities. However, the historical interpretation of the provision and the degree to which that interpretation has subjected Japanese nonprofit organizations to the "permission of the competent authorities" and in particular to the discretion of the competent authorities is rather unusual. It is in fact the most recurrent and pervasive element in the nonprofit legal and operating structure (and is the factor that most distinguishes Japanese philanthropy from that in the United States) and will be explained in more detail in subsequent chapters.

The overlap of government and private initiative in the nonprofit realm was apparent in the organization of the first sizable nonprofit organization pursuant to the dictates of the Civil Code. The On-shi zaidan saisei-kai (Imperial relief association) was established in 1911 at the initiative of the Meiji emperor and with seed money donated by him, to provide medical relief for the poor. Appeals for further endowment funds were conveyed not only to the leading industrialists of the time but also to the prefectural governors.[4]

Throughout the organization's history, it continued to rely on both public and private funding to support its activities.[5]

Between 1915 and 1935, at least ten major private foundations were set up under the provisions of the new Civil Code. The growth in private philanthropic endeavors paralleled the country's rapid industrialization and, in particular, paralleled the growth of the large Japanese corporate conglomerates known as *zaibatsu*. Consistent with the economic goals of the zaibatsu and the emphasis placed by the government on the advancement of science and technology during these years, it is no coincidence that the earliest foundations approved by the government were involved primarily in scientific research and development. These included the Harada sekizenkai, Hattori hokokai, the Asahi Glass Foundation for Industrial Technology, and Mitsui hō'onkai. Although these foundations were private, in the sense that they were established principally with private funds, many were, according to Ms. Kazue Iwamoto (formerly of the Toyota Foundation), established either at the initiative of the government or with the understanding that they would help implement and support national development policies.[6]

In many cases, this "understanding" was supported and solidified by heavy government subsidization of foundation activities.[7] These government subsidies gradually turned into more aggressive interference, thus diluting the "private" nature of the foundations. Official encroachment onto the turf of private organizations reached its peak immediately preceding and during World War II when, because of the exigencies of war, nonprofit organizations were prevailed upon to sacrifice their original agendas in deference to government priorities. In effect, under the emergency war powers measures enacted at this time, most nonprofit organizations lost whatever independent identities they had once had and became mere tools of the government. According to Professor Yujiro Hayashi, "Militarism . . . was then rapidly sweeping through Japan, and the philosophy of repaying debts of gratitude [to society] was steadily twisted into a spirit of offering service to the state."[8]

With their original functions usurped and replaced by wartime exigencies, most of the organizations themselves became superfluous and were either inactive or totally defunct by the end of the war. As a result, these early experiments in private philanthropy had little impact on the postwar development of Japan or on contemporary philanthropy in Japan, other than perhaps in coloring the public perception of the relationship between public-sector and private-sector nonprofit activities.

Decentralization and Fragmentation

Although the war effectively terminated the early nonprofit initiatives themselves, wartime and immediately postwar legal reforms and government priorities have had a lasting impact on the legal system governing nonprofit organizations. One major effect of this wartime restructuring was the decentralization (although not the relaxation) of government control over nonprofit entities, which corresponded to a general decentralization of control over all government functions deemed unessential to the war effort.

As mentioned, the Civil Code provided that nonprofit organizations could be established subject to the approval of the "competent authorities." Before the war, the "competent authorities" were the various ministries of the national government — the Ministry of Science and Technology, the Ministry of Education, the Ministry of Finance — depending on the substantive area of a particular nonprofit organization's activities (e.g., the Ministry of Education is the competent authority for an organization engaged in educational or scholarship activities; see Chapter 4). However, the Approval, Permission, and Extraordinary Measure Acts of 1943 and 1944 to a great extent transferred the responsibility for nonprofit organizations, both their authorization and supervision, to prefectural and local governments.

Initially the transfer of authority was minimal, but as the war accelerated so did the shift in control. The determination of exactly what controls to hand over, and to what extent, was made separately by the individual government ministries involved, but by 1945 the national government ministries collectively had ceded to local authorities control over most nonprofit organizations, except those whose activities were essentially national in scope or importance.

In conjunction with the decentralization in control over nonprofit organizations, significant changes were also made in the general of its people. The government in Japan is referred to, only semi-facetiously, as *okami*, or god ("kami" preceded by an honorific).

The difference, in particular, between Japanese and American attitudes toward government is often cited by Japanese as a major reason for the divergent development of philanthropy in the two countries. As Mr. Yujiro Hayashi pointed out, "the Japanese tend to forget that laws and government are of their own creation and expect public bodies to take responsibility for various aspects of society. Americans, on the other hand, ever since their nation's founding, have felt the need to make up for the deficiencies of the government, with private philanthropy being one outgrowth of this outlook."[23]

The United States is unique in its reliance on the private, non-profit sector to provide necessary social and cultural services. In contrast with many Americans, most Japanese expect and prefer to have government provide for them. The government, too, prefers it that way. One could debate *ad infinitum* which system is "better," and the chances are that Americans would still come out in favor of the private sector and that Japanese would still come out in favor of the government, but the ultimate issue really is "Are society's needs being met in an efficient and humane way?" It would be difficult to say that Japan's are not or that they are being met less well than any other society's needs.

Not only has traditional reliance on government obviated the need and desire for a strong private sector, but it also has created a private sector in which the government plays a large role. As detailed in Chapters 3 through 5, nonprofit organizations are incorporated, licensed, and taxed at the pleasure and subject to the discretion of various branches of the government. Many feel that nonprofit status is conferred grudgingly by the government, which takes the position that "if the activities of these organizations are important enough to merit special status under the law, they are important enough for the government to do by itself without input from the private sector." According to Mr. Mikio Kato, the government's attitude creates a rather circular problem. If the project that a nonprofit organization wants to carry out is deemed important, then the government wants a hand in it; at the same time, once the government steps in, private initiative will languish because people feel that the government is taking care of the matter and is probably best suited to do so in the long run.[24]

20

JAPANESE CORPORATE PHILANTHROPY

Japan As a Middle-Class Society

Another element impeding the growth of the third sector in Japan is the widespread disbelief among Japanese in Japan's current wealth. "Only recently have the Japanese begun . . . to accept the reality that they are not so poor as they used to believe," noted Mr. Osamu Muro, an expert on Third World nongovernmental aid.[25] Even though Japan is now reputed to have more billionaires (per capita) than the United States has and is the home of many of the world's largest companies, the Japanese persist in seeing themselves as solidly middle class and are fond of saying that Japan is a rich country full of poor people.

Undoubtedly the accumulation of large personal and industrial fortunes has contributed to the growth of Japanese philanthropy since the 1960s, much as it did in the United States at the turn of the century, but not as much as it might have if that wealth were generally acknowledged. With respect to individuals, studies conducted in the United States indicate that it is both wealthy people and people who perceive themselves as having sufficient discretionary, disposable income who are the most generous contributors to charitable causes.

A study commissioned by the Rockefeller Brothers Fund and conducted by the Independent Sector in 1986 found that at all income levels, those who believed that they had discretionary income gave more generously to charity than did those who did not. The study further found that those who reported they had little or no worry about money needs in the future were also more generous contributors.[26] Both of these observations have implications for giving in Japan where—due to the high price of land and housing and the absence of a social security system to defray the costs of retirement—most Japanese save assiduously, do not feel they have large amounts of discretionary income, and worry greatly about their financial reserves for the future.

Notes

1. Yujiro Hayashi, "Toward Japanese Philanthropy," quoted in *The Future of Private Grant-Making Foundations*, Proceedings of the Tenth-Anniversary International Symposium of the Toyota Foundation (Tokyo: Toyota Foundation, 1985), p. 62.

2. Shichihei Yamamoto, "Contract Versus Consensus," in *Entrepreneurship: The Japanese Experience*, vol. 3 (Kyoto: PHP Institute, 1982), p. 3.

3. Chie Nakane, "Organizational Comparison Between Japanese and Southeast Asians," in *In Search of Meaningful Cultural Exchange: Southeast Asia and Japan* (Tokyo: Japan Foundation, 1980), pp. 169–170; and Shichihei Yamamoto, "Consanguineous and Territorial Societies," in *Entrepreneurship: The Japanese Experience*, vol. 2 (Kyoto: PHP Institute, 1982), pp. 1–4.

4. Yamamoto, "Consanguineous and Territorial Societies," p. 7.

5. Hayashi, "Toward Japanese Philanthropy," p. 60.

6. In the United States, individual philanthropy is the base from which corporate philanthropy derives. Although corporate philanthropy in the United States has grown dramatically since it first became acceptable in the mid-1950s, 85 to 90 percent of the total dollar amount dedicated to charitable causes in most years comes from individuals, whereas only 4 to 5 percent comes from corporations.

7. In particular, individual initiatives have been noteworthy and on the rise in the realm of nongovernmental organizations (NGOs). Although the total size and number of these development organizations are still extremely small—270 NGOs in all—more than 30 percent have been established by private citizens' groups with largely or wholly private funds. See *Directory of Non-Governmental Organizations in Japan: NGO's Active in Development Cooperation* (Tokyo: Japanese NGO Center for International Cooperation [JANIC], 1988).

8. As quoted in Amy Borrus et al., "Japan Digs Deep to Win the Hearts and Minds of America," *Business Week*, July 11, 1988, p. 39.

9. *A.P. Smith Mfg. Co. v. Barlow*, 97 A. 2d 180 (Super. Ct. N.J. 1953), *affirmed*, 98 A. 2d 581 (S. Ct. N.J. 1953), *appeal dismissed*, 346 U.S. 861 (1953).

10. In this regard, it is interesting to note that until 1936, companies could deduct gifts to charities only if they qualified as business expenses. With the amendment in 1936 of what is now Section 170 of the Internal Revenue Code, companies were relieved of the burden of proving the business purpose of their gifts. For a two-year period, corporations could make contributions and deduct them as either charitable contributions or business expenses. Then in 1938, the Internal Revenue Code was once again amended, this time to deny corporations the right to deduct charitable gifts as business expenses. This was intended to emphasize (perhaps unrealistically) the "pure," altruistic motives of corporate giving, but according to Boris Bittker, it mainly serves as a reminder of the business context in which such gifts are actually made. See Boris Bittker, "Charitable Contributions: Tax Deductions or Matching Grants?" *Tax Law Review* 28 (1972), pp. 57–58.

11. Of course, it is also likely that there is less soul-searching because the topic as a whole does not merit much attention in Japan; accordingly, people have not focused on defining an appropriate role for corporate philanthropy. Those who do concern themselves with the issue have for the most part accepted the view popular in the United States of "enlightened self-interest" as the impetus and justification for corporate philanthropy.

12. Interview with Mr. Hideo Yamaguchi, April 28, 1987.

13. Discussions with Mr. Tom Fox, October 16, 1986.

14. Sometimes giving within an industrial association is anonymous and sometimes participants are known, but either way, the donor has the security of having done what was appropriate in the eyes of the group.

15. Among the earliest foundations were Kan'onko (meaning, roughly, "Society of gratitude") established in 1827; Saito hō'onkai (Hō'onkai translates as "Society for repaying gratitude"), established in 1923; and Mitsui hō-onkai, established in 1934.

16. Approximately 70 percent of the foundations that I interviewed for this book were established on the occasion of an anniversary of the company's founding.

17. Interview with Mr. Mikio Kato, associate managing director, International House of Japan, March 16, 1987.

18. Details of interview withheld at the request of the interviewee.

19. In the Japanese language, pronouns, adjectives, and verb conjugation vary according to the sex and status of the person being spoken to or spoken about, in relation to oneself.

20. Yamamoto, "Consanguineous and Territorial Societies," p. 1, quoting political scientist Naoki Komuro; and Yamamoto, "Contract Versus Consensus," p. 1.

21. Yamamoto, "Contract Versus Consensus," p. 1.

22. Although such administrative guidance often has the force of law, it is not issued through formal, legally dictated channels. There is, in fact, very little statutory authority for issuing such guidance.

23. Yujiro Hayashi, "The Role of Private Philanthropy in Japan," in *The Role of Philanthropy in International Cooperation*, Report on the JCIE 15th Anniversary, International Symposium (Tokyo: Japan Center for International Exchange, December 1985), p. 5.

24. Interview with Mr. Mikio Kato, March 16, 1987. Mr. Kato cited the Japan Foundation (see the discussion of the Japan Foundation in Chapter 5) as a prime casualty of this circular logic. Initially, the Japan Foundation, established at the initiative of the Foreign Ministry, was to have received half of its funding from the government and half from the private sector, but once the government had funded its half, the private sector withdrew. To this day, the foundation has received very little funding from private

sources, but it does receive designated donations from private business that it then channels to the specified donees.

25. Jackson, "Charities Go Begging."

26. In 1984, 34 percent of those responding to the Independent Sector survey who reported that they had moderate to large amounts of discretionary income gave an average of $1,120, compared with $510 for the 49 percent of respondents who reported that they had a small amount of discretionary income, and $250 for the 27 percent of respondents who reported that they had no discretionary income. See *The Charitable Behavior of Americans*, Findings from a National Survey (commissioned by the Rockefeller Brothers Fund) (Washington, D.C.: Independent Sector, 1986).

3

The Development of
the Nonprofit System

Economic growth and prosperity in Japan have led to an increased concern with and ability to provide for social welfare. At the same time, political pressure and the growing diversity of society have begun to alter traditional perceptions of what constitutes social welfare and by what means it ought to be looked after.

Social welfare, or social activities in the public interest, is normally provided through three different channels — public institutions (i.e., the government or its agencies), private profit-making institutions (corporations), and private non-profit-making or voluntary organizations — each of which has its own means and ends. In the case of profit-making organizations, activities are conducted primarily for economic gain, but indirectly, social welfare is advanced through research, provision of products and services, and employment. In the case of both government and nonprofit organization activities, the public good is more directly advanced (targeted), but while the government's motivation is essentially political, the voluntary organization's motivation is thought to be humanitarian or charitable.

The balance among these three different mechanisms and their degree of separation from one another varies from society to society and constitutes one of the major distinctions between Japan and the United States and, in particular, between Japanese and U.S.-style philanthropy. Japan has been, remains, and will probably continue for the foreseeable future to be much more reliant on government-provided services (and on corporate-provided services) than the United States is. I alluded earlier to some of the reasons for this. In addition, as mentioned in Chapter 2, the boundary between

24

government and other nonprofit organization activities in Japan often is not clearly delineated.

Nonprofit organizations in Japan run the gamut from wholly private to almost wholly public, that is, government sponsored, funded, and controlled. Truly private, "charitable" nonprofit organizations—those that generally correspond to the U.S. category of 501(c)(3) charitable organizations—such as the corporate foundations that are the focus of this book, are a relatively new and very small subset of the total group termed nonprofit.[1] In the minds of the public (and often in the view of the government), the distinction between private and other nonprofit organizations is not at all clear, which has created some misperceptions and negative perceptions about the nature and function of private philanthropy in Japan.

In order to place private philanthropy and private foundations in their proper historical and legal context, this chapter will briefly trace the development of the nonprofit sector as a whole and then will separate out that group of private organizations relevant to this study.

The Civil Code and *kōekihōjin*

As in Europe and the United States, the earliest nonprofit organizations in Japan were religious—Buddhist temples and Shinto shrines—which, in addition to their religious activities, offered a variety of social and educational services. There is evidence of this type of activity in Japan as early as the eighth century and continuing through the Edo period (1603–1868) in the form of fund-raising to build temples and support for private education.

Toward the end of the Edo period, in 1829, the Akita kan'on ko (*kan'on* means gratitude; see Chapter 2), regarded by most as the first organized private philanthropic organization in Japan, was established by a merchant serving a lord in the Akita domain. This organization offered help to poor farmers, sought to alleviate the financial distress of the domain, and supported orphaned children. According to historical records, approximately two hundred people in the region joined together and pooled their funds to purchase a piece of land that served as an endowment supporting the organization's activities.[2]

Despite this interesting example, the shogunate as well as the provincial lords of the Edo period were the main providers for the public welfare. Their highly centralized, tightly controlled system of government left little room for, and gave little encouragement to, the development of privately sponsored public-benefit initiatives. The more contemporary concept of nonprofit organization really began with the concerted modernization of Japan during the Meiji Restoration, beginning in 1868, and with the passage of the current Civil Code in 1898.[3]

Article 34 of the Civil Code states: "An association or foundation relating to worship, religion, charity, science, art or otherwise relating to public interests and not having for its object the acquisition of gain may be made a juristic person subject to the permission of the competent authorities." This provision, like most of the Japanese Civil Code, is closely modeled on the German Civil Code (especially the draft of 1888) and incorporates that law's reliance on administrative approval and supervision of private, nonprofit initiatives, something that did not exist in relation to the early Buddhist organizations.

The provision itself is not unique. Nonprofit organizations around the world exist at the pleasure of the relevant governing authorities. However, the historical interpretation of the provision and the degree to which that interpretation has subjected Japanese nonprofit organizations to the "permission of the competent authorities" and in particular to the discretion of the competent authorities is rather unusual. It is in fact the most recurrent and pervasive element in the nonprofit legal and operating structure (and is the factor that most distinguishes Japanese philanthropy from that in the United States) and will be explained in more detail in subsequent chapters.

The overlap of government and private initiative in the nonprofit realm was apparent in the organization of the first sizable nonprofit organization pursuant to the dictates of the Civil Code. The On-shi zaidan saisei-kai (Imperial relief association) was established in 1911 at the initiative of the Meiji emperor and with seed money donated by him, to provide medical relief for the poor. Appeals for further endowment funds were conveyed not only to the leading industrialists of the time but also to the prefectural governors.[4]

Throughout the organization's history, it continued to rely on both public and private funding to support its activities.[5]

Between 1915 and 1935, at least ten major private foundations were set up under the provisions of the new Civil Code. The growth in private philanthropic endeavors paralleled the country's rapid industrialization and, in particular, paralleled the growth of the large Japanese corporate conglomerates known as *zaibatsu*. Consistent with the economic goals of the zaibatsu and the emphasis placed by the government on the advancement of science and technology during these years, it is no coincidence that the earliest foundations approved by the government were involved primarily in scientific research and development. These included the Harada sekizenkai, Hattori hokokai, the Asahi Glass Foundation for Industrial Technology, and Mitsui hō'onkai. Although these foundations were private, in the sense that they were established principally with private funds, many were, according to Ms. Kazue Iwamoto (formerly of the Toyota Foundation), established either at the initiative of the government or with the understanding that they would help implement and support national development policies.[6]

In many cases, this "understanding" was supported and solidified by heavy government subsidization of foundation activities.[7] These government subsidies gradually turned into more aggressive interference, thus diluting the "private" nature of the foundations. Official encroachment onto the turf of private organizations reached its peak immediately preceding and during World War II when, because of the exigencies of war, nonprofit organizations were prevailed upon to sacrifice their original agendas in deference to government priorities. In effect, under the emergency war powers measures enacted at this time, most nonprofit organizations lost whatever independent identities they had once had and became mere tools of the government. According to Professor Yujiro Hayashi, "Militarism . . . was then rapidly sweeping through Japan, and the philosophy of repaying debts of gratitude [to society] was steadily twisted into a spirit of offering service to the state."[8]

With their original functions usurped and replaced by wartime exigencies, most of the organizations themselves became superfluous and were either inactive or totally defunct by the end of the war. As a result, these early experiments in private philanthropy had little impact on the postwar development of Japan or on contemporary philanthropy in Japan, other than perhaps in coloring the public perception of the relationship between public-sector and private-sector nonprofit activities.

Decentralization and Fragmentation

Although the war effectively terminated the early nonprofit initiatives themselves, wartime and immediately postwar legal reforms and government priorities have had a lasting impact on the legal system governing nonprofit organizations. One major effect of this wartime restructuring was the decentralization (although not the relaxation) of government control over nonprofit entities, which corresponded to a general decentralization of control over all government functions deemed unessential to the war effort.

As mentioned, the Civil Code provided that nonprofit organizations could be established subject to the approval of the "competent authorities." Before the war, the "competent authorities" were the various ministries of the national government—the Ministry of Science and Technology, the Ministry of Education, the Ministry of Finance—depending on the substantive area of a particular nonprofit organization's activities (e.g., the Ministry of Education is the competent authority for an organization engaged in educational or scholarship activities; see Chapter 4). However, the Approval, Permission, and Extraordinary Measure Acts of 1943 and 1944 to a great extent transferred the responsibility for nonprofit organizations, both their authorization and supervision, to prefectural and local governments.

Initially the transfer of authority was minimal, but as the war accelerated so did the shift in control. The determination of exactly what controls to hand over, and to what extent, was made separately by the individual government ministries involved, but by 1945 the national government ministries collectively had ceded to local authorities control over most nonprofit organizations, except those whose activities were essentially national in scope or importance.

In conjunction with the decentralization in control over nonprofit organizations, significant changes were also made in the general administrative mechanisms by which local governments were controlled by the central government. As a result, with a few exceptions, local governments not only received control over nonprofit organizations but also were free to set their own standards for approving the establishment of such organizations and were able to grant such approvals without consulting the central government. In most cases, all that was required was notice to the appropriate authorities in Tokyo.

This decentralization persists today and is one of the salient features of the nonprofit system. In fact, as of March 1985 (the latest date for which accurate statistics are available) out of approximately 21,000 nonprofit entities organized under the Civil Code, only 6,000 are authorized by national government agencies; the balance of 15,000 are under the control of local government agencies.[9] In addition, from 1971 to 1985, the rate of increase in the number of organizations sponsored by local agencies was about four times that of organizations sponsored by national agencies.[10]

A second major effect of the wartime and postwar legal reforms was the proliferation and fragmentation of laws relating to nonprofit organizations. Specifically, numerous pieces of special legislation were passed establishing nonprofit corporations of a highly public nature. Some of these laws, such as the Japan Red Cross Society Act, were unique and targeted to a single organization, whereas others were generic, authorizing the establishment of numerous corporations under a single category. Examples of the latter type include the Social Work Act (1938), the Medical Service Act (1948), the Social Education Act (1949), the Library Act (1950), and the Religious Corporation Act (1951).

Both types of law in effect created a system of nonprofit organizations that ran parallel to, and frequently intersected with, the legal system established by the Civil Code. As a result, today there are essentially three separate legal mechanisms according to which a nonprofit organization may be established in Japan. For ease of reference, I will call these (1) targeted legislation, (2) generic legislation, and (3) Civil Code.

First, a nonprofit organization may be created by a specific, targeted piece of legislation such as the legislation that created the Japan Foundation in 1972. These organizations are largely public in nature and are referred to as special public corporations, or *tokushuhōjin*. They are listed by name in an appendix to the Corporate Tax Law and, in terms of the American experience, are probably most similar in concept to the National Endowment for the Arts or the National Endowment for the Humanities. Although these organizations may reap some support from private funds, they are predominantly supported by the government.

Second, nonprofit corporations may be licensed under the provisions of more generic legislation such as the Private School Law, the Religious Corporation Law, and the Social Welfare Service Law. Organizations established under this type of generic legislation may include those set up with purely government funds, purely private funds, or some combination of both.

Under both of these mechanisms — targeted and generic legislation — the legal procedures and requirements for establishing, operating, and governing the corporation are determined by and are particular to the piece of enabling legislation. However, the system is complicated by the fact that some of these special laws, such as the Red Cross Society Act of 1951[11] and most of the generic legislation, incorporate and adopt the Civil Code provisions either in whole or in part.[12] Thus, these two types of specially legislated nonprofit corporations may themselves be divided between those that are for legal purposes set up under the Civil Code and those that are set up completely outside and parallel to the Civil Code according to the organizational and operational provisions of the particular piece of enabling legislation. (If this all seems baffling, it is only because it is presenting an accurate view of what is a baffling, intricate, and interwoven system.)

In either case, what is important to remember is that many (probably most) of the nonreligious organizations created by either targeted or generic legislation are established at the initiative of the government rather than at the behest of the private sector and that such organizations constitute the bulk of the nonprofit organizations existing in Japan today.[13] According to Mr. Katsuo Kumagai of the Hitachi Corporation, "Many of these so-called private organizations have a quasi-political aim. They are in fact set up to do — under contract or otherwise — the work of the government or work that the government wants to see done but, for one reason or another, not by itself."[14]

The third means of creating a nonprofit organization in Japan is by utilizing the provisions of Article 34 of the Civil Code.[15] It is under this provision that most of the truly private nonprofit organizations, corresponding most closely to the U.S. private foundations, are established and operated. It is estimated that today there are approximately 21,000 such organizations in Japan. Of these, the vast majority are operating foundations. There are thought to be between 1,000 and 3,000 grant-making foundations in Japan, of which only 200 are of any significant size.[16] This book will focus on this small subset of private, grant-making organizations and on the Civil Code, tax, and operational provisions applicable to them. Nonetheless, an awareness of the multiplicity of forms that nonprofit organizations may assume in Japan is important for a variety of reasons.

First, many of the quasi-governmental nonprofit organizations formed under special legislation perform some of the charitable functions that in other countries (notably the United States) private organizations might perform, thus obviating to some degree the need for private philanthropy, although not, as some have mistakenly assumed, negating the existence of a philanthropic spirit in Japan.

Second, the blurred definitions and boundaries between public, quasi-public, and private nonprofit organizations have created confusion among Japanese people about the nature and function of private philanthropy and private philanthropic organizations. Most of the Japanese I encountered were not familiar with the term *kōekihōjin* (which means, literally, "public-benefit juristic person" and is the closest equivalent in Japanese to the term *nonprofit organization*), and those who were, somehow associated the activities of these organizations with the government — often cynically so. For example, many think of *kōekihōjin* as organizations to which older government officials are sent for rather cushy, postretirement employment. This, indeed, is a well-known practice in special public corporations and occurs much more rarely in private foundations, but in the public mind little distinction is made.[17]

This confusion itself has a dampening effect on the growth of private initiatives, for there is a healthy degree of cynicism about the true public concern of many government politicians and officials (as amply demonstrated by the public reaction to the stock and sex-related scandals that plagued the Japanese government in 1989) and there is also a disincentive to get involved and to participate when the assumption is that the government is already involved. Mr. Mikio Kato of the International House of Japan cited this factor as the main reason that the Japan Foundation, originally intended to be funded 50 percent by the government and 50 percent by private enterprise, remains today a mostly government-funded organization. Once the government stepped in, companies could no longer see the need for, or benefit from, their own participation.[18]

Finally, the overlap of government and private roles in the non-profit area has had a subtle, residual effect on private organizations' perceptions of themselves and their role in relation to government and society as a whole. As discussed in the next chapter, even in the realm of private organizations, the government has a great deal of indirect control and influence, owing to the tremendous discretion it is given by the Civil Code in overseeing the formation of such organizations. Although many private organizations are beginning to protest such a high degree of government involvement, to some extent their own self-image seems influenced by the overflow of government into nonprofit areas. Without really questioning why, many organizations have adopted a limited scope of activities for themselves, assuming that certain substantive areas are more appropriately addressed by government alone. Interestingly, in the United States, many foundation experts feel that one of the most important roles that foundations can and should play is that of evaluating government institutions, programs, and policies.[19] Admittedly, this is a creative and forward-looking view of the role of private foundations, and it probably partakes more of the ideal than of the real; nonetheless, it is not a concept that I heard expressed with respect to potential roles for Japanese foundations. I believe that the still-prevalent view of the government as *okami* (see Chapter 2) and the involvement of government in establishing private organizations make this vision difficult to conceive in Japan at present. That is, it is the government that oversees and supervises private initiatives, not the other way around.

Notes

1. The term 501(c)(3) organizations is shorthand for those organizations listed in Section 501(c)(3) of the Internal Revenue Code and exempt from federal income tax under both that provision and Section 170 as

"charitable" organizations. As is the case in Japan, these organizations do not reflect the full range of nonprofit organizations that can be legitimately established in the United States. They do, however, represent the sole category to which tax-deductible contributions can be made, as explained more fully in Chapter 5.

2. See Tanaka Minoru, *Kōeki hōjin to kōeki shintaku* (Public interest corporations and public interest trusts) (Tokyo: Keisho shoin, 1980).

3. The Civil Code was actually legislated in 1896 but not enforced until 1898.

4. Hayashi Yujiro, *Nihon no zaidan* (Private philanthropy in Japan) (Tokyo: Chūō kōronsha, 1984).

5. The Saiseikai still exists as a Civil Code organization, but its original functions have been almost entirely replaced by the government. With the passage of the Medical Protection Act of 1941 and the Livelihood Protection Law of 1946, the government has taken over the responsibility of providing medical care for the poor.

6. Kazue Iwamoto, "An Overview of Japanese Philanthropy and International Cooperation in the Third World," in Kathleen D. McCarthy, ed., *Philanthropy and Culture: The International Foundation Perspective* (Philadelphia: University of Pennsylvania Press, 1984), p. 122.

7. I was in fact told that at one time a prerequisite for being able to set up a nonprofit organization under the Civil Code was receipt of a government subsidy.

8. Hayashi, "Toward Japanese Philanthropy," p. 65.

9. The 21,000 organizations referred to here as Civil Code organizations are those that correspond most closely to the U.S. concept of private foundations. In fact, there are over 220,000 organizations incorporated under Article 34 of the Civil Code, but at least 200,000 of these were formed under special legislation that incorporates the provisions of the Civil Code. Many of these latter organizations are either religious or quasi-public entities.

10. Note that the number of national government agencies also includes those organizations authorized by local branches of the national agencies, so that the number of those organizations under local control is in excess of 15,000. Takako Amemiya, Shoin joshi tanki dai-gaku kiyō, Vol. 3 (Tokyo: Shoin joshi tanki dai-gaku, 1987), pp. 204–209.

11. In fact, the Japanese Red Cross was originally established under the Civil Code in 1900 as a private nonprofit association, but revisions in its charter and status made by the Japanese Red Cross Society Act of 1951 brought it more into the public realm. Another example of a Civil Code organization with "public" status is the Japan Broadcasting Corporation (NHK), a Civil Code nonprofit organization whose budget is determined every year by the Diet and that is accordingly closely supervised by the Diet.

12. According to a report issued in 1985 by the Management and Coordination Agency of the prime minister's office, as of the end of 1983 there were approximately 11,000 social welfare corporations, 6,000 private school corporations, and 183,000 religious corporations set up under generic legislation but operating under Civil Code provisions and therefore listed as Civil Code organizations.

13. There are no statistics available on the breakdown between truly private organizations and quasi-public organizations. However, there seems to be universal agreement among the people I interviewed that in one way or another, most of the nonprofit organizations operating in Japan today are in some large measure linked to the government.

14. Interview with Mr. Katsuo Kumagai, general manager, secretary's office, Hitachi Corporation, November 21, 1986.

15. In addition to Civil Code organizations, the law also provides for a system of charitable trusts. As explained in Chapter 5, these trusts are, for most purposes, treated by law like Civil Code organizations and perform similar public-interest functions (the main difference being that they are not considered juridical persons). Because to date, so few charitable trusts have been formed and because they are so similar to Civil Code organizations, references in this book to Civil Code organizations include charitable trusts as well.

16. Unlike the United States, where the majority of private foundations are grant-making foundations, estimates for the total number of grant-making foundations in Japan vary from 1,100 to 3,000, or 5 to 15 percent of the total number of Civil Code corporations. See the survey conducted by the Foundation Library Center of Japan, 1986.

17. According to a report by the Council of Governmental Special Corporation Employees (*Seirokyo*) issued in 1987, as of late 1986, 77.5 percent of executive positions at special public corporations (*tokushuhōjin*) were held by former high-ranking bureaucrats. Of such bureaucrats retiring from their special corporation posts between November 1985 and October 1986, 133 out of 142 received retirement allowances of ¥20 million (approximately $140,000 at an exchange rate of ¥140/$1). See "Ex-bureacrats [*sic*] hold 77.5% of top posts at special corporations," *Japan Times*, April 5, 1987, p. 2. This practice and its lucrative rewards continue despite a cabinet recommendation calling for restraint on such *amakudari* with respect to special public corporations. The practice of *amakudari* (literally meaning "descent from heaven") is not confined to special public corporations. It is common practice for retired government bureaucrats to receive lucrative appointments in private corporations with whose supervision they were closely involved during their years in government service.

18. Interview with Mr. Mikio Kato, March 16, 1987.

19. See, for example, Commission on Foundations and Private Philanthropy (Peterson Commission), "Recommendations to Foundations," in *Foundations, Private Giving, and Public Policy* (Chicago: University of Chicago Press, 1970); and Waldemar Nielson, "The Roles of Private Grantmaking Foundations in American Society," in *The Future of Private Grantmaking Foundations*, Proceedings of the Tenth-Anniversary International Symposium of the Toyota Foundation (Tokyo: Toyota Foundation, 1985), p. 25.

4

Establishing a Foundation—
Law and Practice

The first and most important thing to be said about the Civil Code law governing private philanthropy and private philanthropic organizations in Japan is that far from providing exhaustive, detailed, and definitive rules, it offers merely a skeletal framework and a basis for guidance. Substance is given to the framework by the more informal practices and discretionary choices of the various government agencies whose responsibility is to administer the nonprofit provisions of the law.

Of the approximately fifty distinct provisions of the Civil Code relevant to nonprofit organizations, only a handful are targeted directly to them. The balance are articles of general application to corporations of any kind, formed pursuant to the Civil Code. This forms a startling contrast with the United States, where the typical not-for-profit corporation law of each of the fifty states contains dozens if not hundreds of rules designed specifically for nonprofit corporations. The same could be said of the tax law applicable to nonprofit organizations.

Some of the reasons for the relative lack of legal emphasis on the nonprofit sector in Japan I covered in Chapters 1 and 2. First, private nonprofit organizations in Japan are quite new, a product of the postwar era and particularly of the post-1960s era. They have not yet become a critical force in Japanese society and therefore have not warranted much attention. More importantly, Japanese society in general is much less reliant on legal relationships and strict legal constructions than is American society (and for that matter, most Western societies). It organizes itself mainly along the more fluid lines of personal relationships, interlocking debts of *on* (obligation) and *giri* (gratitude), and the concept of consensus reached through discussion and compromise. Finally, the latitude left to government to fill in the blanks left by a sketchy legal structure is reflective of a traditional Japanese willingness to rely on and defer to governmental discretion and wisdom in making choices and providing for social well-being. This is true not only in the nonprofit realm but also in the for-profit realm, where the "Japan, Inc." collaboration of government and private enterprise has been widely (perhaps too widely) analyzed and discussed.

Because the legal system and the practices that implement it are so radically different in Japan from those familiar in the United States—the U.S. system is highly centralized, the Japanese is highly decentralized; the U.S. system is mechanical and standardized, the Japanese is fluid and *ad hoc*—it is useful to review briefly and compare the U.S. system before describing the nonprofit incorporation procedures in Japan.

In the United States, the procedure for establishing and obtaining tax benefits for a charitable, nonprofit entity, regardless of the nature and scope of its activities, is fairly uniform and almost completely nondiscretionary and consists of two separate and distinct steps: incorporation under state law and receipt of tax-exempt status from the Internal Revenue Service (IRS).

Incorporation under the nonprofit corporation law of any of the fifty states is a mechanical application and a formal approval exercise.[1] Articles of incorporation and other documentation are submitted to the appropriate state offices, and if the documents are properly prepared and meet legal requirements, the application is approved. The procedure is, for the most part, equivalent to the incorporation procedure followed by for-profit organizations.

Once an organization has obtained corporate status, it applies to the IRS for tax-exempt status. This, too, is a mechanical procedure. If the application meets the legal requirements set forth in the Internal Revenue Code (IRC), the application will, and in fact must, be approved, and the organization will be exempt from federal income taxes. Moreover, if the organization is a "charitable" organization in accordance with the IRC (Sections 501 and 170), it will become eligible to receive contributions that can be deducted by the donors for federal income tax purposes. In tax matters, the states follow the IRS. Once the organization is tax exempt under federal law, it generally receives corresponding benefits under state law. Nothing could be more different from the Japanese system, in which there is not one procedure but many, in which incorporation and tax status procedures overlap, and in which discretion is the major operative force.

According to Article 34 of Japan's Civil Code of 1934, nonprofit corporations may be established "subject to the permission of the competent authorities." The determination of which government agency is the appropriate "competent authority" depends on the substantive area of the organization's activities and the geographical area in which those activities will be carried out. Thus, an organization conducting local educational or scholarship activities would apply to the local branch of the Ministry of Education, whereas an organization conducting national-level educational activities would apply directly to the Ministry of Education; an organization engaged in international projects would apply to the Ministry of Foreign Affairs; and an organization involved in activities that were both international and educational (e.g., international exchange programs) would probably have to apply to both the Ministry of Education and the Ministry of Foreign Affairs.[2]

Although, as discussed in more detail later, there has been some effort to standardize the approval process among the different national and local ministries, each is still basically free to set its own standards and requirements, and local government agencies can do so without consulting or even informing a national ministry. Moreover, even within a given government agency, the standards may vary on a case-by-case basis. The Japanese system is truly an "approval" system. Accordingly, the application procedure is not purely mechanical, and the authorities may and do use tremendous discretion in granting or withholding approval.

Finally, unlike the United States, the incorporation and tax status procedures for nonprofit organizations in Japan are not neatly separated. The ministry that has authority to grant corporate nonprofit status also has the authority to make the organization exempt from both national and prefectural income tax (this is true even for local government agencies), and the two are handled simultaneously. Tax-exempt status is an automatic consequence of being incorporated as a nonprofit entity.

This granting of tax-free status requires no consultation with the Ministry of Finance or with the National Tax Administration (the NTA, a division of the Ministry of Finance). By contrast, the ability of an organization to receive contributions that will be tax deductible by the donor, is strictly controlled by the Ministry of Finance and is largely subject to its discretion.

The consequences of all this decentralization and discretion are numerous. First, the lack of centralization makes it almost impossible to get an accurate picture of the actual current status of philanthropy in Japan. There is no single clearinghouse for information of even the most straightforward sort, such as the total number of nonprofit organizations in Japan, the numbers of operating foundations versus grant-making foundations, and the total amount of charitable contributions made in any year. More detailed or sophisticated information is correspondingly more difficult to obtain. Mr. Korenobu Takahashi, director of corporate and scientific programs for IBM Japan, related that when he attempted to conduct a survey of corporate philanthropic activity before designing a domestic-giving program for IBM Japan, he was unable to find out which companies were giving, in what substantive areas, or in what magnitude.[3] The dearth of readily available information makes the researcher's task difficult, and it also makes supervision and oversight of the nonprofit sector problematic for the government.

Second, the diversity and discretion inherent in the system eviscerate almost any attempt to generalize about the incorporation procedure or predict the outcome of any particular incorporation application. "What is the procedure for becoming a nonprofit organization in Japan?" "It depends on which ministry's guidance you fall under." "Is it easy to become a nonprofit organization in Japan?" "Well, it depends on which ministry you talk to." "How long does the incorporation procedure take?" "It depends on which ministry is supervising you."

The lack of predictability in the incorporation process often has a debilitating effect on smaller, private nonprofit initiatives. Whereas large companies can marshal the resources to decipher and master the system, smaller endeavors are often stymied at the start, not knowing where or how to begin and not able to commit time and money to a process whose outcome is so uncertain. This perpetuates the overwhelmingly corporate makeup of the foundation sector in Japan and also the perception that such organizations are largely the tools of government and/or of business.

With this background in place, in the remainder of this chapter I shall set forth the law, such as it is, and describe the incorporation procedure, such as it may be.

The Law – Its Provisions and Analysis

Article 34 of the Civil Code states: "An association or foundation relating to worship, religion, charity, science, art or otherwise relating to public interests and not having for its object the acquisition of gain may be made a juristic person subject to the permission of the competent authorities." Thus the provision describes two types of organizations (associations and foundations), defines their function ("relating to public interest" and not focused on gain), and delineates a procedure for their establishment.

In addition to the two types of Civil Code organization cited, Japanese law also provides for a system of charitable trusts. The trust differs from Civil Code associations and foundations in that instead of forming a new corporation or association, a donor or group of donors designates an existing individual or corporation (in Japan as in the United States, this usually is a trust bank) as trustee for transferred assets. The trustee is then responsible for managing the assets and carrying out the trust's charitable purpose. Although this system was first provided for under the Trust Law of 1922, the first charitable trust was not established until 1977. Today there are between 220 and 240, compared with approximately 21,000 Civil Code charitable organizations.[4]

For most legal purposes, charitable trusts are treated similarly to Civil Code organizations. Under Article 66 of the Trust Law, they too must be organized for the public benefit, must not have gain as their purpose, and must seek official approval for their establishment. For tax purposes as well, charitable trusts are largely indistinguishable from their Civil Code counterparts. Because of their overriding similarities and relatively scant numbers, I shall discuss charitable trusts together with charitable corporations, and references to charitable corporations under the Civil Code will include charitable trusts except where otherwise indicated.

The two types of *kōekihōjin*, or public-benefit corporation, defined by the Civil Code are distinguished by whether the corporation is a group of people associated to serve a public purpose (a *shadan hōjin*, or incorporated association) or whether it is a body of assets dedicated to a given public-interest function (a *zaidan hōjin*, or incorporated foundation). Like for-profit corporations, both the charitable association and the charitable foundation are organized under a governing instrument called the Articles of Association and Articles of Endowment, respectively. These are the basic rules defining the organization, function, and management of the entity and must set forth its objectives, formal name, location of offices, assets, and other pertinent information such as the names and titles of members of the board of directors, voting requirements, and terms for the entity's dissolution.[5]

The main difference between the two types of organization is the flexibility with which they carry out their public-interest functions. An incorporated association consists of a group of members whose general assembly must meet at least once a year. This general assembly has decision-making authority over all the affairs of the association, including modification of the Articles of Association (and hence modification of the association's activities) and dissolution of the organization. Decisions by the general assembly are executed by the directors of the organization and overseen by the auditors. By contrast, the incorporated foundation's purpose is fixed by the Articles of Endowment. The activities of the foundation's directors must be carried out within this framework and can be modified, at least in theory, only through reapplication to the competent authorities.

A second, more practical difference is the ease with which the two types of organizations can obtain approval from the government. Because it must have an endowment that is deemed sufficient by the appropriate government ministry (in some cases this can represent a significant capital commitment), a foundation is likely to undergo more legal formalities and a higher degree of government scrutiny than an association is, which requires merely the joining together of a like-minded group of individuals.[6]

Legal theory and government preferences aside, the functional differences between these two types of charitable corporations are largely conceptual. Some associations have an endowed fund and some foundations have associate members. Some associations make it fairly difficult to revise their articles of association, while some foundations provide for easy revision of their charters. For tax purposes, as well, the two types of organization are essentially indistinguishable.

Regardless of which legal form the charitable corporation takes, Article 34 stipulates that the organization must be related to the public interest and must not have financial gain as its object. According to Mr. Shumpei Tomono, executive director of the Japan Association of Charitable Corporations, this language is overly vague and hence is problematic. "The Civil Code is ninety years old, and this provision has remained virtually unchanged during all that time, so that it no longer matches today's changed situation. Article 34 says only that the *kōekihōjin* must be related to the public interest, but that term is not defined. Many organizations 'related to' the public benefit are not necessarily directly for the public benefit. The difference among these types of organizations gets wider and wider, yet they are treated identically under the law, especially the tax law."[7]

As Mr. Tomono's comment indicates, neither the Civil Code nor the tax law distinguishes among nonprofit organizations those that are truly for the public interest and those that are not. This is in direct contrast with the provisions of U.S. law that distinguish these public-interest, charitable organizations — the so-called 501(c)(3) organizations — from other nonprofit organizations by their treatment for federal income tax purposes. Not only are 501(c)(3) organizations exempt from income tax (as are other non philanthropic, nonprofit organizations), but they also are eligible to receive tax-deductible contributions (which others are not). In order to receive these double benefits, however, the organization must be both organized and operated for charitable purposes.[8]

Japanese law, too, provides that public-interest organizations are both tax exempt and eligible to receive deductible contributions, but it merely requires that the organization be "related to" the public interest in order to reap those benefits.[9] Thus, as Ms. Takako Amemiya pointed out, many "neutral" organizations such as alumni associations and unions, which are nonprofit but organized primarily for the benefit of their members, have qualified under Article 34 as nonprofit public-interest corporations eligible to receive tax-deductible contributions. "It is a defect of the legislation," observed Ms. Amemiya, "that there is no other legitimate way to establish a non-public-interest and non-profit-making corporation."[10]

This defect in the legislation has led to the incongruous inclusion of the Sumo Wrestling Association, the Japan Motor Boat Racing Association (the latter is essentially a gambling association), and various local parking lots and golf courses in the roster of public-interest organizations eligible to receive tax-deductible contributions. Virtually everyone with whom I discussed philanthropy in Japan cited these organizations as the outstanding examples of the vast latitude with which the phrase "related to the public interest" has been interpreted, a latitude that has led in many cases to skeptical public opinion about the nature of public-interest "philanthropic" organizations.

Article 34 states that a charitable corporation must be related to the public interest, and it also must not have gain as its objective. Nonetheless, nonprofit organizations in Japan are permitted to engage in business activities, and unlike the United States, there is no requirement that these business activities be related to the organization's charitable purpose, nor are there any requirements or restrictions regarding the expenditure of business profits.[11]

Many *kōekihōjin* operate simultaneously both a for-profit and a nonprofit enterprise. Although this practice is sanctioned by the law, it has been abused in the past, and the potential for abuse remains. In theory, *kōekihōjin* are kept from running amuck under the liberal provisions of the Civil Code because their establishment and operation is subject to the scrutiny of the "competent authorities." In accordance with Article 34, an organization seeking to incorporate is required to submit an application for official approval (this application includes the Articles of Association or Endowment as well as other documentation) to the agency of the appropriate level of government that exercises jurisdiction over the types of activities that the applicant wishes to conduct.

Although Article 34 grants authority to the various agencies of government to approve and oversee nonprofit entities, it does not prescribe any procedures for doing so. This, as well as the determination of what is to be contained in the written application, is generally left to internal directives issued by the ministries themselves. Numerous attempts have been made to standardize the procedures used by the various government agencies, but to date none has been completely successful.[12] Accordingly, it is extremely difficult to describe accurately the exact procedures to be followed in incorporating a foundation under the Civil Code. Perhaps the only generalization that can be made is that regardless of the ministry chosen and regardless of that ministry's particular requirements, the written application is merely the formal end product of a long negotiation between the nonprofit entity and the government agency. What follows is a general outline of the steps in such a negotiation, obtained from interviews with many foundations.

Establishing a Foundation — Practicalities

The first step in incorporating a nonprofit organization is for the organization to determine which of the competent authorities is the appropriate overseer. This is not as simple a matter as it might appear. As discussed earlier, the choice of ministry is not prescribed by law but, rather, depends on both the substantive and geographic scope of the organization's activities and, to a certain extent, on the organization's assessment of which ministry will look upon its application most favorably. Only those organizations whose activities are national or international in scope apply directly to a national government agency. All others apply to a branch of local or prefectural government (or in some cases to the local branch of one of the federal government agencies).

Today, most nonprofit organizations in Japan are incorporated under the auspices of local government agencies. It is estimated that of the approximately 21,000 Civil Code organizations, approximately 15,000 are under the competency of local authorities.[13] This should not be surprising, for there are at least 45 "competent authorities" at the local level, compared with 22 at the national level. In addition, most organizations confine their activities to a limited geographic area, negating the necessity for national supervision.[14]

Mr. Kiyoshi Segami, director and secretary general of the Inamori Foundation in Kyoto, further suggested that one reason for the prevalence of locally based organizations is the relative ease with which approval can be obtained.[15] This would appear to be a logical consequence of the fact that at local levels the ties between businesses and the government agencies that supervise them are often quite close. Because the granting of nonprofit status is discretionary, the approval process can be facilitated if the ministry involved has direct familiarity — through personal relationships or otherwise — with the applicant. In addition, the relatively small size and circumscribed activities of local nonprofit organizations in many cases obviates the need for the detailed scrutiny to which the more ambitious national organizations may be subjected.

In any case, once the appropriate level of government has been determined, the appropriate branch of government must be selected, one whose substantive area of control matches the substantive activities of the nonprofit organization. Thus an organization conducting local educational activities, for example, would apply to the local branch of the Ministry of Education (or to the prefectural equivalent), whereas an organization conducting national educational activities would apply directly to the Ministry of Education; an organization engaged in international projects would apply to the Ministry of Foreign Affairs; and an organization involved in activities that were both international and educational (e.g., international exchange programs for students) might have to apply to both the Ministry of Education and the Ministry of Foreign Affairs.

This process is not as clear-cut as these examples make it appear. To begin with, there is a certain amount of forum or agency "shopping." That is, frequently, an organization's proposed activities will fall within the possible jurisdictional realm of any one of several government ministries. In such a case, either the organization will choose a ministry with which it has a close business relationship, or it will "shop" in order to select the ministry that it believes will be most receptive to its application. This belief may be based on objective or subjective criteria.

For example, there is a general consensus among representatives of philanthropic organizations (particularly those with an international focus) that the Ministry of Foreign Affairs is rather liberal, supportive, and innovative in its approach to nonprofit organizations. By contrast, the Ministry of Education is perceived as being tough, conservative, narrow, and loath to cede control to private organizations.[16] Accordingly, if a choice can be made (as in the case of an international student exchange program), an organization will opt to submit its incorporation application to the Ministry of Foreign Affairs and will hope to escape notice by the Ministry of Education.

On the more subjective side, an organization may choose to make its application to a particular ministry on the strength of personal relationships between the founding organization and some individual in the ministry, rather than solely on the basis of the organization's substantive activities. The personal connection is often pivotal, as the ministries lack definitive objective standards by which to assess an application. Thus a process that in one case may take two years, can, with the assistance of a well-placed personal contract, be completed within six months.

Unfortunately, it is not always possible to shop for ministries successfully, as government agencies are under no obligation to sponsor any particular petitioning organization. Establishment of a nonprofit organization is not a matter of right; rather, it is a matter of choice on the part of the government as well as the organization. Accordingly, many organizations are turned down by their first-choice agency (no explanation need be given) and have to look elsewhere, often tailoring their programs in the process to match the jurisdictional scope of the second- or third-choice ministry.

As indicated earlier, if an organization's activities are multidisciplinary, it may have to seek the approval of several ministries simultaneously. Although almost all of the foundations that I interviewed were unanimous in their view that they would avoid this alternative if at all possible, one dissenting voice pointed out that in some cases, joint agency supervision may be preferable because it avoids excessive interference by a single agency. "It is a matter of power dynamics observed anywhere. While two dogs fight for a bone, a third runs away with it."[17]

Perhaps the biggest problem with joint supervision is the delay and confusion it causes in the incorporation procedure. Each ministry has its own prerequisites, requirements, and procedures, and in some cases these may conflict, or at least do not dovetail, with the prerequisites, requirements, and procedures of another ministry. At the very least, the overlap of authority means that more people must ultimately be consulted, cajoled, and persuaded. The incorporation of a nonprofit entity is not a mechanical procedure. It is a long process of discussion, negotiation, consultation, and compromise that merely becomes longer and more tedious as more parties are drawn into it.

In addition, interagency power plays, turf battles, and jockeying for position can have a significant impact on the nonprofit organization that forms the playing field. For example, more than one foundation related the following type of story:

> We were at the point of discussing foundation board members with Ministry A. They suggested that we include on our board several people, including a former vice-minister of Ministry A. This is a fairly common practice, and because we had no particular objection to that individual, we agreed. We then returned for further discussions with Ministry B. When they saw our proposed list of board members, including the former member of Ministry A, they suggested that we add to our board a particular individual who was at that time an official of Ministry B. Until that point, such a thing had never been discussed, and now we have too many bureaucrats on our board.

Efforts on the part of nonprofit entities to avoid the ill effects of joint agency supervision have a chilling and restrictive effect on the range of activities they are willing and able to pursue. Because multidisciplinary foundations, by definition, fall within the jurisdiction of multiple ministries, organizations tend to have a single purpose, with those corporations wishing to pursue diverse activities setting up separate foundations in each field of interest. Thus the Hitachi Corporation has established six separate foundations in Japan under the jurisdiction of six separate government agencies and is pursing activities ranging from rehabilitating prisoners to assisting scientific research.[18] Unfortunately, following Hitachi's course means frequently undergoing the incorporation process — with its attendant costs in time, money, and frustration — a daunting prospect for most foundation organizers.

For organizations that insist on pursuing a multidisciplinary course, overlapping ministerial jurisdiction may be unavoidable.[19] This is particularly true of high-profile organizations like the Inamori Foundation, whose activities are of a type to attract and appeal to ministry attention. The Inamori Foundation is a Kyoto-based foundation established by the Kyocera Corporation and by its founder Mr. Inamori with an endowment of ¥5 billion (approximately $35 million). Its main activity is awarding prizes to individuals for outstanding achievement in the fields of mathematics, basic sciences, performing arts, and advanced technology; accordingly, it was formed under the joint auspices of three ministries of the national government, the Ministry of International Trade and Industry (MITI), the Ministry of Education, and the Ministry of Science and Technology. The foundation's organizers were well aware of the difficulties inherent in pursuing a multifaceted program but felt that they could not split the organization into thirds because "that would express the wrong sentiment. Mr. Inamori is an engineer who loves poetry and art. He wanted the foundation to reflect the best from the fields of science and art."[20]

Even when the multidisciplinary aspects of an organization's activities are less apparent, interagency competition and rivalry, for which the vertically organized Japanese government is well noted, frequently result in joint supervision. According to Mr. Hachiro Koyama, president of the Japan Fulbright Foundation, "Sometimes, after you make your application to one ministry it becomes impossible to escape the notice of a rival ministry. Although there is no formal mechanism whereby one ministry can learn of your organization's application to another, there are informal means. One is the media."[21]

Illustrating Mr. Koyama's statement is the case of a relatively new foundation involved in international educational exchange. It first sought the endorsement of the Ministry of Education, which rejected its application. Subsequently, on the basis of a personal contact with an official in the prime minister's office, the organization was able to elicit the support of that agency. After an article about the fledgling foundation appeared in the local press, both the Ministry of Education and the Ministry of Foreign Affairs contacted the foundation and the prime minister's office, expressing interest and seeking a piece of the pie. At that time, the foundation had not yet been formally incorporated, and so the matter was resolved by granting a measure of joint jurisdiction.

The Inamori Foundation's situation was similar. Having applied to MITI for nonprofit status, it came to the attention of the Ministry of Education and the Ministry of Science and Technology after articles about the proposed foundation appeared in the press. In the case of the Asahi Glass Foundation, after functioning for many years under the auspices of MITI, it suddenly came to the attention of the Ministry of Education, which even at that late date requested, but was not granted, joint oversight responsibility.[22]

Choice does not end with the selection of a supervising ministry but, rather, continues through the determination of who or what department within a given ministry will be responsible for reviewing an organization's application for nonprofit status. As far as can be determined, none of the ministries of the national or prefectural governments have separate divisions for dealing with nonprofit organizations, either for the initial application review and approval or for subsequent monitoring.

To the extent that there is a general procedure for assigning an application within a ministry, it operates approximately as follows: An organization interested in becoming a *kōekihōjin* is first sent to the *sōmuka*, the equivalent of the general secretary and chief administrative officer for the agency. On the basis of the *sōmuka*'s assessment of the substantive area of the organization's work, the application is assigned to that division of the ministry with the appropriate expertise. Thus, an organization sponsoring comparative economic research, for example, might be assigned to the economics division in the Ministry of Foreign Affairs.

Once again, the procedure is not as neat as this description might indicate, for the *sōmuka* may also evaluate an application based on his assessment of its relative level of importance (a determination that in turn is based on factors such as the size and importance of the sponsoring company and any relationship existing between the sponsoring company and the agency) and assign it, accordingly, to someone higher or lower on the totem pole in the ministry. Moreover, the whole *sōmuka* referral system may be circumvented and approval procedures accelerated if the organization has a direct personal connection in the ministry. Thus in the case of the Fulbright Foundation, a former Fulbright fellowship recipient then working in the prime minister's office facilitated that organization's application and approval process. Similarly, the sponsors of a foundation named for a retired diplomat directly approached the diplomat's former colleagues at high levels in the Ministry of Foreign Affairs and skirted entirely the normal, slower channels.

After an appropriate government agency and the appropriate person or division within the agency are identified, the process of actually structuring the organization begins. This involves essentially two procedures: first, a laborious series of consultations, negotiations, and compromises and, second, the submission of a formal written application memorializing the agreement molded in that process.

How are these consultations and negotiations conducted, and how is a consensus reached? This is a topic that has incessantly intrigued students of Japan and Japanese culture. Whole books have been written on the subject, so anything written here will merely be scratching the surface. However, perhaps the most important point to be made is that even using the term *negotiation* is probably misleading if it conjures up images of the quasi-adversarial, confrontational style of negotiation familiar in the West. Japanese negotiations, of course, do contain elements of confrontation, but at least with respect to the incorporation of a nonprofit entity, the Japanese term *nemawashi* more accurately describes the process.

Nemawashi means literally "digging around the roots of a tree," but in this context it refers to a method of consensus building in which various responsible parties are probed and pushed informally and repeatedly for their reaction to the proposals of the entity seeking incorporation. These proposals are then recast to reflect the informal government reactions, so that by the time a written application is finalized, formalized, and submitted for approval everyone knows essentially what to expect.[23]

In the context of the nonprofit incorporation procedure, *nemawashi* can be bothersome, but it also serves several valuable functions. First, because the law gives very little direction to the organization and so much of the incorporation process is left to the discretion of the government, *nemawashi* enables an organization to get a clearer sense of what the particular ministry actually requires in terms of legal documentation, assets required to be committed to the nonprofit function, and the like and even to influence what the ministry ultimately will require. On the flip side, it enables the ministry to probe and to test the sincerity and authenticity of the organization and also in some cases to influence the organization's choice of activities and board members. Almost all of the foundations that I interviewed for this book had at least one board member who was either currently or formerly a member of the ministry, or ministries, responsible for its supervision. All of this government involvement is not negative per se, but it does raise some questions about just how private some of these "private" initiatives really are.

The governmental need to substantiate the veracity of the organizations is, according to many I talked to, critical. Of course it would be whenever a benefit — tax exemption — is being awarded by the government and is subject to possible abuse, but the wariness of the government in Japan and the means by which the government assuages its fears seem to be part and parcel of a very Japanese system.

Certainly, there have been in the past and continue to be nonprofit organizations that abuse their tax benefits.[24] However, most of the NTA, the Ministry of Finance, and the foundation personnel with whom I spoke did not cite tax abuse as a major problem.[25] Instead, the real concern of the government, according to Mr. Mikio Kato, is that "anything important enough to be given tax-favored status by the Japanese government is important enough that the government itself should be doing it."[26] Thus, the detailed scrutiny of nonprofit organizations stems not so much from fear of tax abuse as from a deep-rooted reluctance to mete out tax benefits and thereby to assist private organizations to perform functions that government could — and, in the perception of many, should — perform.[27]

The method used to establish an organization's authenticity is also peculiarly Japanese. It is based as least as much on confidence in the individuals involved as on the objective merits of a proposal (see the discussion of *on* and *giri*, in Chapter 2), and this is why face-to-face *nemawashi* or negotiation is key. The amount of *nemawashi* required will itself vary depending on who the organization's sponsors are and how much their reputation precedes them in the particular ministry. Thus in a case reported to me, a foundation whose chief sponsor was a former prime minister was established with very little to do, whereas a foundation whose stated purpose was virtually identical but whose sponsors were not prominent former politicians went through a two-year runaround before finally being approved.[28]

Another important function served by the back-and-forth *nemawashi* system is that by facilitating compromise in advance it obviates the need for unseemly confrontation during the formal approval process. No one on either side loses face by either having to reject a proposal or having to be rejected.[29] Ideas are discussed and modified outside the conference room, as it were, so that by the time everyone gathers round the table, the formalities can be accomplished smoothly. This is another manifestation of the individual versus the group discussed in Chapter 2. Confrontation, by definition, disrupts a unified group appearance. In Japan, such disruptions tend to take place, if at all, behind tightly closed doors. The end product of successful *nemawashi* is a united, seemingly harmonious "group"-oriented decision.

This group decision is reflected in the written application documents submitted to the ministry for formal approval. Even when describing the written application, it is very difficult to generalize about the requirements and standards for review because they are set by each ministry separately and accordingly vary from ministry to ministry and also within a single ministry, on a case-by-case basis. Despite the resulting diversity, the Japan Association of Charitable Corporations, in its *Handbook for Non-Profit Organizations*, identified six documents that seem to be required by all ministries as part of the written application:

1. Statement of the organization's public purpose.
2. Bylaws.
3. Written plan of activities (usually covering a two-year period).
4. Financial plan (usually covering a two-year period).
5. List of assets.
6. List of board members.

While the final documents are being reviewed, the ministry normally issues a temporary approval of the organization as a *kōekihō-jin*.[30] At this point an organization may begin its operations. The temporary approval is valid for between three and six months, during which time the ministry has a chance to observe the organization in action and to verify further to its own satisfaction the accuracy of the information contained in the application before issuing final approval.

According to Mr. Shumpei Tomono, executive director of the Japan Association of Charitable Corporations, although the standards for application review imposed by and within the ministries are not uniform, the concerns expressed by government officials are fairly consistent. Does the organization have a true public purpose and the means to carry out that purpose? Are the organization's proposed activities feasible given the budget allocated? Is the budget appropriately allocated? Are the organization's assets (endowment) sufficient? Does the organization have appropriate status and management through the proposed members of the board of directors?

Again, there are no fixed guidelines according to which these concerns can be measured, and the relative importance attached to each varies, often in accordance with the type of organization. For example, many agencies have specified a minimum capital amount necessary for establishing a foundation, today approximately ¥200 million to ¥300 million, according to Mr. Tomono.[31] However, whereas the Department of Culture of the Ministry of Education may deem this capital endowment to be critical to the establishment of a nonprofit art museum, it may relax or waive the requirement entirely in the case of a cultural exchange or other program whose capital demands are less intense.

Mr. Tomono also cited the status of an organization's board members and organizers as a factor weighing heavily in the review process and influencing the importance attached to other factors. Thus, for example, if the ministry has confidence in the fundraising energy and ability of the board members, it will attach less weight to the organization's initial capital endowment. For organizations conducting international programs, Mr. Tomono felt that confidence in the organization's members is often the determining factor, because in the government's view this type of activity requires "a genuinely internationally minded person who understands the role of private organizations and how to make them succeed."[32]

Mr. Tomono and others also pointed out that in setting their review standards, government officials are often influenced by their own past experience. That is, they tend to examine new applications with an eye toward the types of organizations and activities they believe to have been successful in the past and also with an eye toward maintaining their own autonomy and influence.

All of the consultations, discussions, compromises, and tradeoffs involved in successfully completing the incorporation procedure take vast amounts of time and energy, the major complaint of those who have undergone the process. The time from the submission of the written application alone until its final approval can take as much as a year. Including the preapplication negotiation time, the whole process can take as much as two or three years (or as little as six months with the proper connections), with the average probably being a year and a half.[33]

Smaller organizations, in particular, that lack high-placed connections to smooth the way are often discouraged and deterred by the sheer laboriousness of the endeavor. They are loath to invest resources in a project whose outcome is so unpredictable because of these amorphous, arbitrary, and discretionary standards. The arbitrariness of the system is perhaps best illustrated by a conversation I had with a former Japanese government official. This gentleman had developed an interest in nonprofit organizations and was exploring the possibilities of setting up a small foundation to assist foreign scholars in Japan. As we talked, I lamented the fact that it was so difficult and time-consuming to get such an enterprise launched in Japan. To my surprise, he looked at me in total bewilderment and burst out, "But it's so simple . . . if you know the right people!"[34]

Case Study

The actual machinations of the complex and varied incorporation procedure can perhaps best be explained by using a case study. The Ushiba Memorial Foundation, named for a former ambassador to the United States, Nobuhiko Ushiba, was formally established on October 13, 1986, approximately one and a half years after the founders first approached the Ministry of Foreign Affairs. According to Mr. Hiroshi Takaku of the Japan Center for International Exchange (JCIE), which processed the application on behalf of the Ushiba Foundation, "The single most important factor in the whole process was ministry and individual discretion."[35]

Because the foundation intended to conduct activities in the field of international affairs and because Ambassador Ushiba himself had been part of the Ministry of Foreign Affairs, that agency was approached as the appropriate competent authority. After several "informal" discussions, the JCIE made an official visit to the *sōmu-ka* (general secretary). The individual who was the *sōmuka* at the time was not particularly receptive to the proposal for the foundation, and so he imposed rather stiff conditions:

> First he said that we would need a minimum ¥200 million endowment before the foundation could be approved. This put us in a terrible position because corporations won't contribute that kind of money unless they have an assurance that the contribution will be fully tax deductible, but you can't get a ruling from the Ministry of Finance about tax deductibility until the organization is incorporated.[36] Second, after receiving an inquiry about starting a foundation, the *sōmu-ka* is supposed to assign the organization to another department in the ministry to handle the application details. He ultimately assigned us to the economics division, but as he took his time doing so, we lost a few months right there.[37]

Then, fortuitously, the *sōmuka* was replaced, and the man who filled the position was a powerful figure in the Ministry of Foreign Affairs and a friend of former Ambassador Ushiba. Accordingly, he was in favor of the foundation and was in a position to help further its cause. His first action was to check with the ministry's legal division regarding the necessity of such a large initial endowment. Informed that this was a discretionary, not a legal, requirement, he promptly lowered the amount to ¥50 million. This figure, according to Mr. Takaku, was reached because it was the amount that the JCIE felt confident about being able to collect in advance of the Finance Ministry's determination about tax deductibility.[38]

With this major obstacle surmounted and the assistance of a friendly *sōmuka*, the rest of the incorporation procedure went rather smoothly. In a major departure from normal practice, the *sōmu-ka* even gave the JCIE a copy of a previously submitted application for a successfully incorporated foundation to use as a model. "This was a big surprise and a big help," said Mr. Takaku, "because usually you get no help with the written application. What happens is that you submit it and it's returned for the correction of two typographical errors, and then you resubmit it and it is sent back for minor revisions, *ad nauseam*. Of course, it did take us six meetings before we were able to convince anybody to give us a model to work from."[39]

The final application for the Ushiba Foundation was submitted on September 15, 1986, and official approval was received less than a month later. Although the process took a year and a half of concerted effort, the JCIE estimated that had there not been a change of *sōmuka* in midstream, the incorporation might very well have dragged on for at least another year.

Postformation Government Supervision

Despite the difficulty and complexity of forming a nonprofit organization, once formed, the entity encounters little interference from government in the way of oversight or continuing supervision. Similar to foundations in the United States, nonprofit organizations must file annual information reports containing financial and program summaries of the past year's activities. In addition, they must submit a proposed budget and program plan for the coming year. Although many foundations indicated that the preparation of these reports was cumbersome and time-consuming, the reports themselves seem to be largely formalistic and rarely challenged.

In addition to this official method of screening foundation activities, the presence of a ministry official or officials on the board of most entities adds a supplementary supervisory mechanism. Despite this, there has been a continuing problem over the years with dormant foundations. *Dormant foundations*, as the name implies, are those that have ceased to function as foundations but whose corporate shell and nonprofit designation continue to exist on the books and continue to have value because of their attendant tax benefits. In 1979, after negative media publicity about dormant foundations, the Civil Code was amended to permit competent government agencies to withdraw the nonprofit charter of any organization that "remains inactive for three or more consecutive years without a lawful reason."[40]

To the extent that the dormant foundations exist merely as paper companies, performing no activities, they are not a problem. However, they do present some temptation for tax and other abuses. As discussed in the next chapter, the profit-making activities of non-profit organizations are taxed at a rate lower than the normal corporate tax rate; hence any business activities continued under, or transferred to, the nonprofit shell can (in theory) improperly take advantage of this reduced rate.

Dormant foundations also have advantages besides pure tax advantages. For example, several dormant foundations have been "purchased": in some cases as a means of avoiding tax and in others as a means of establishing a new nonprofit entity without having to undergo the time-consuming and irritating process of seeking ministry approval. The purchaser merely takes over the defunct entity (presumably by paying the founders) and gives it new life and activity. Not only does this scheme save time; it also saves money. Reportedly, purchasers have been able to acquire dormant foundations for a fraction of the ¥200 million to ¥300 million amount that most ministries now require as capital endowments for new foundations.

Although the issue of dormant foundations was consistently cited to me as one of the principal problems plaguing the nonprofit system, the numbers of organizations involved does not appear to be that large. A 1985 inspection conducted by the Management and Coordination Agency revealed 172 national and 403 local foundations that had not submitted their required information reports since 1983 and accordingly were considered by their respective supervising ministries to be not substantially performing their nonprofit functions.[41] Part of the discrepancy between the perceived scope of the problem and the figures compiled by the Management and Coordination Agency may have to do with the definition of dormant foundations. That is, it is quite conceivable that there are in fact foundations that have ceased their major charitable functions but that nonetheless continue to file information reports in order to retain their nonprofit status for other purposes.

What is clear, though, is that all of the decentralization and discretion involved in the administration of the nonprofit system, combined with the fact that there is very little computerized record keeping for either information or tax purposes (as mentioned in the next chapter there are no social security or taxpayer identification numbers in Japan to facilitate computer record keeping, auditing, and cross-checking) makes adequate oversight difficult and undoubtedly contributes to the abuses that do exist, no matter what their scale.

Notes

1. Although each of the states has its own not-for-profit corporation law, the substance of these laws does not vary dramatically from state to state. More importantly, in all states the procedure is largely formalistic and is not significantly different from that prescribed for regular business corporations.

2. Many states also require in their nonprofit laws that the Department of Education approve the incorporation of an educational entity or that the Department of Health and Human Services approve the establishment of a social welfare organization, but again this is a rather mechanical process. If the documents are properly prepared and submitted, the incorporation must be approved.

3. Interview with Mr. Korenobu Takahashi, director of corporate and scientific programs, and Mr. Masahiko Masuda, manager of corporate programs, IBM Japan, November 11, 1986.

4. The reasons for the slow launching of the trust system are several. First, at the time the law regarding charitable trusts was adopted, the trust mechanism in general was not well known in Japan. Like charitable corporations, trusts were to be approved and administered by various ministries of government depending on the substantive areas of the trusts' activities, but because the ministries themselves were not familiar with the trust as a legal entity, until the mid-1970s, most of them did not adopt any sort of internal guidelines for dealing with trusts. The catalyst for change in the seventies was a study of nonprofit organizations initiated by the prime minister's office in response to negative publicity surrounding nonprofit organizations in general, many of which had ceased to perform their public benefit functions and were instead using their favored tax status for private gain. At the request of the prime minister's office, the Japan Association of Charitable Corporations, together with various trust banks and the Trust Company Association of Japan, formed a study group that was instrumental in explaining to the various government ministries the concept and function of the charitable trust. The ministries, in turn, were then able to begin adopting internal guidelines for the trust approval process.

Although these organizational guidelines began to be implemented in the 1970s, there were no specific rules dealing with the taxation of charitable trusts until 1987. The income tax law (Article 11, Clause 3) had provided tax exemption for trust income, but there was no specific provision granting tax-exempt status to trusts. This was mainly a technical oversight, and so trusts formed prior to 1987 were, de facto, given tax-exempt status by extension of the laws governing charitable corporations; nonetheless, the lack of an explicit exemption may have discouraged the formation of additional trusts. Finally, as experience in the United States indicates, charitable trusts may be the preferred mechanism of individuals, but they are not widely employed by corporations, which tend to prefer to establish foundations in corporate form. Because most philanthropy in Japan is corporate, it is not surprising that the corporate-form foundation has been preferred to the charitable trust.

5. Civil Code, Article 37 (incorporated association), and Civil Code, Article 39 (incorporated foundation).

6. Even though associations are theoretically easier to establish, as of March 1985 the breakdown between foundations and associations was just about equal, approximately eleven thousand incorporated foundations and ten thousand incorporated associations under the Civil Code. Not surprisingly, all of the grant-making organizations that are the focus of this book are incorporated foundations. As a result, I tend to use the term *foundation* when discussing issues equally applicable to incorporated associations.

7. Interview with Mr. Shumpei Tomono, executive director, Japan Association of Charitable Corporations, September 25, 1986.

8. Although some have found this language redundant, the legislative history and other commentary on IRC Section 170 make it clear that the purpose of such language is to avoid the problem cited by Mr. Tomono. A 501(c)(3) organization must be established with charitable activities as its purpose, and it must actually carry out those purposes in order to maintain its nonprofit status and receive the tax benefits provided by law.

9. Japanese law also permits certain unincorporated associations and foundations dedicated to the public benefit to be exempted from income tax as long as they do not have profit as their goal and they designate an administrator or representative. Many voluntary organizations operate in this form at least until they are able to become incorporated. However, in noncorporate form, these organizations risk unlimited liability for their members and representatives. In addition, although they may be considered tax exempt, they are not eligible to receive tax deductible contributions.

10. Amemiya, "Present Situation and Problems" p. 199. Recommendations to modify the law to accommodate some type of intermediate nonprofit organization that would be tax exempt but not eligible to receive deductible donations have been advanced by the Japan Association for Charitable Corporations and by the Liaison Conference for the Guidance and Control of Non-Profit Public Interest Corporations, established by the prime minister's office in 1985, but to date no action has been taken. The

latter body actually has issued a policy recommendation that the following types of organizations should not be considered as having public-interest goals: (1) mutual friendship, liaison, and membership discussion groups such as alumni or hobby associations; (2) welfare and mutual aid groups only for members of a specified industry or profession; and (3) moral or economic support groups for an individual, such as a supporters' association.

Although the members of the Liaison Conference are representatives of the various government ministries that supervise nonprofit organizations, the recommendations issued by the conference do not have the force of law and are advisory only. In addition, although the policy statement indicated that these types of organizations should not be considered "public interest," it stopped short of suggesting that such organizations — in particular existing organizations falling into those categories — should be denied the right to receive tax-deductible contributions.

11. Although from now on these organizations will be called *nonprofit* organizations, that term was borrowed from the U.S. lexicon. The direct translation of *kōekihōjin* (the Japanese term) is "public profit" or "public benefit." The word itself contains no implication that the organizations must be nonprofit, only that they be geared toward the public benefit. In fact, the restriction in Article 34 that organizations must not have gain as their objective has been interpreted to mean not that the entities may not seek a profit but that they may not share such profits among their members. The practical effect of this interpretation is explained in Chapter 5, but note here that even in the United States, where the term *nonprofit* is widely used, the main restriction on such entities is a prohibition on the distribution of profits, not on the earning of profits. These prohibitions are usually contained in the state laws under which the organizations are chartered.

12. The Liaison Conference for the Guidance and Control of Non-Profit Public Interest Corporations succeeded the Liaison Conference for the Control of Non-Profit Public Interest Corporations, originally formed in 1971 at the initiative of the prime minister's office with the purpose of standardizing the procedures for establishing and supervising nonprofit Civil Code organizations. The original group consisted of the section chiefs of those bureaus in each ministry that were most closely related to nonprofit activities. (Today the reconstituted conference consists of the general secretaries of each ministry. At present, the general secretary's office seems to be the *madoguchi*, the "window," or first point of contact for most organizations seeking nonprofit status.) These section chiefs focused on four major areas of concern: (1) issues regarding the establishment of nonprofit organizations, (2) issues regarding the supervision of nonprofit

organizations, (3) standardized accounting procedures, and (4) the problem of defunct or "dormant" organizations. Some progress has been made in each of these areas. In particular, guidelines have been drawn up with respect to the documentation required to apply for nonprofit status, as well as annual information reporting and accounting procedures. It seems that for the most part, these guidelines are followed, but as they do not have legal effect, they are sometimes honored in the breach.

13. Amemiya, "Present Situation and Problems," p. 204–210.

14. This type of local focus is characteristic of U.S. corporate philanthropy as well. According to a report issued in 1984 by the Taft Corporation, more than 75 percent of corporate contributions in the United States are made to local and regional organizations rather than to national or international causes. The Taft report quotes a statement by the Norton Company in its 1982 *Social Investment Report*: "Business people can be expected to know how to run a business; they shouldn't be expected to know how to run a country. . . . [We] do believe, however, that within our plant communities — which we know and understand — and with the advice of our employees, we can have a significant impact by making social investments thoughtfully and carefully." The Taft report also points out that for most companies, the local community is their marketplace. The general public that makes up the communities are, or may be, the consumers of the company's goods and services. It should not be surprising, then, that corporations, whether directly or through foundations, would choose the local community as the target for their charitable giving.

15. Interview with Mr. Kiyoshi Segami, director and secretary general, Inamori Foundation, and Mr. Yasushi Futamatsu, deputy secretary, Inamori Foundation, August 1, 1986. Mr. Segami observed that patronage and political maneuvering play a large role in the incorporation of locally based charitable organizations and that consequently abuses of the nonprofit system among such locally based organizations are common. He cited specifically the example of profitable local parking lot and golf course "foundations."

16. The Ministry of Education, in general, has a reputation for being rather conservative and inward focused. One gentleman suggested to me, however, that another reason for that ministry's reluctance to encourage nonprofit activity is that already over fifteen hundred Civil Code nonprofit organizations are under its direct supervision. Interview with Mr. Hiroshi Miyabashi, research officer of the management office, prime minister's office, November 11, 1986.

17. Conversation with Mr. Akira Iriyama, executive director, Sasakawa Peace Foundation, May 23, 1988.

18. According to Mr. Kazuo Kumagai, Hitachi would have preferred to establish only one or two general-purpose foundations, but the restrictions of the current legal regime made that impossible. Interview, Mr. Kazuo Kumagai, general manager, secretary's office, Hitachi, Ltd., November 21, 1986.

19. It also is occasionally possible to establish a multidisciplinary foundation under the auspices of the prime minister's office, as is the case with the Toyota Foundation and the Nippon Life Insurance Foundation, but the prime minister's office is rather selective, having at this time perhaps only sixty such organizations under its direct supervision.

20. Interview with Mr. Kiyoshi Segami, August 1, 1986. Mr. Segami observed that in the case of the Inamori Foundation, because initial application was made to MITI, which is the most powerful of the three agencies and is, in George Orwell's words, "more equal" than the others, MITI has had more impact on the foundation's development than the other two agencies have.

21. Interview with Mr. Hachiro Koyama, president, Japan–United States Educational Exchange Promotion Foundation (Fulbright Foundation), March 20, 1987.

22. Interview with Dr. Tsuneo Okamura, executive secretary, and Mr. Isao Ono, managing director, Asahi Glass Foundation for Industrial Technology, October 7, 1986.

23. The ritualistic nature of the final, formal incorporation was brought home to me when in late 1986 I attended the incorporation ceremony and first board meeting of the Ushiba Foundation. Several officers of the foundation were scheduled to speak and formally accept their appointments. Details of the ceremony had been decided in advance among foundation and government representatives, and the acceptance statements had already been prepared. Essentially, the meeting had been rehearsed. But then one member, instead of reciting his rehearsed lines, indicated some reluctance to take up his post, and everyone else at the meeting was thrown completely off guard by this unexpected divergence from the norm.

24. In 1971–1972 these abuses received a great deal of media coverage, and as a result a prime minister's office task force was assigned to study reforms of the entire legal system governing nonprofit organizations.

25. This in itself is interesting, for at the end of every tax year, news articles abound, indicating that quite to the contrary there is tremendous tax abuse in the nonprofit realm. It is not clear whether the NTA and Ministry of Finance officials with whom I spoke with were unaware of the problems or just unwilling to talk about them.

26. Interview with Mr. Mikio Kato, March 16, 1987.

27. One representative of the Nippon Life Insurance Foundation told me that when his company first approached the Ministry of Finance about setting up a foundation (it approached the Finance Ministry because this ministry regulates the activities of life insurance companies generally, but it was ultimately chartered by the prime minister's office owing to the foundation's multidisciplinary scope), the ministry's reaction was that if the company had so much excess profit available for "discretionary" use, it should just lower its insurance premiums rather than endow a foundation. Interview with Mr. Nobuaki Mochizuki, executive director and secretary general, Nippon Life Insurance Foundation, August 2, 1986.

28. The importance of personal relationships is not unknown in the nonprofit world in the United States either, but instead the influence of such relationships is felt in the realm of awarding grants, selecting board members, and choosing philanthropic causes (see Chapter 6). It is wholly absent from the mechanical process of establishing a nonprofit entity.

29. In fact, there is no legal provision for appealing a rejected application, nor, according to Mr. Tomono and Ms. Amemiya, is a ministry required or expected to give reasons for rejecting an application. When I asked Mr. Tomono about statistics on rejected applications, he explained that there were no such statistics because even the rejection of an application is somewhat informal. In general, an organization gets a sense during *nemawashi* as to how its application is being received. If the feeling seems to be negative, then the proposal is reformulated, if possible, or a new sponsoring ministry may be sought. Thus, according to Mr. Tomono, it is highly unlikely that any organization would get very far into the approval procedure only to find out suddenly that its application had been turned down with no explanation.

30. According to Mr. Hiroshi Takaku of the Japan Center for International Exchange, by the time the final application forms are submitted, all the major issues have already been agreed upon, and so approval is automatic. What is not automatic, however, is obtaining formal *hanko*, or seals, representing the consent of various departments within the government agency, without which approval is not official.

The affixing of *hanko* in Japan is equivalent in the West to having a legal document notarized. Each Japanese has his or her own distinctive *hanko* which must be registered with a local government ward office in order to be valid legally. When the equivalent of a notarized signature is necessary, the signatory must obtain from the appropriate ward office a certificate attesting to the validity of his or her *hanko*. Different ministries have different requirements concerning how recently that certificate of authenticity must have been issued to be considered valid (usually not more than one to three months before the date of the transaction for which the *hanko* is required). Thus, in a situation such as the approval of a nonprofit organization, for which *hanko* are required from many individuals (often representing departments that have had nothing to do with the incorporation procedure), a domino effect of delays can occur if one individual's certificate of validity expires before another's can be obtained. The difficulty of obtaining valid *hanko* was consistently (and somewhat humorously) cited as an irritating by-product of the whole bureaucratic approval process. Mr. Seiichi Mitani, executive director of the Mitsubishi Bank Foundation, noted that it added at least a month to the approval time for his organization.

31. According to Mr. Tomono and others, this creates the rather circular problem that an endowment is needed to set up the foundation but that the issue of whether and to what extent the endowment donation will be tax deductible cannot be resolved until nonprofit status is granted. This is not so much of a problem in the case of a foundation to be endowed by a single corporation, but it can be a major obstacle to the formation of foundations that require a broader fund-raising effort.

32. Interview with Mr. Shumpei Tomono, September 25, 1986.

33. This does not include the receipt of rulings regarding the deductibility of contributions to the organization, which can take another six months to a year. In addition, the process can be unintentionally delayed by the annual staff reassignments that routinely take place in all government ministries. It is quite common in the Japanese bureaucracy for officials to hold their posts for no more than two years and then to be rotated into a completely new division where they may have to begin from scratch mastering the subject matter. Thus, both for-profit and nonprofit entities frequently have to cope with delays while recently assigned officials become acquainted with their new turf.

34. Interview with Mr. Eiichi Furukawa, July 13, 1987.

35. Interview with Mr. Hiroshi Takaku, Japan Center for International Exchange, November 11, 1986.

36. See Chapter 6. Actually, informal inquiries and discussions of tax deductibility often are conducted simultaneously with the incorporation process, even though an official determination on the matter cannot be made until after incorporation is accomplished. In the case of the Ushiba Foundation, consultations with the Ministry of Finance regarding deductibility of contributions took place throughout the approval process.

37. Interview with Mr. Hiroshi Takaku, November 11, 1986.

38. In order to arrive at this figure, the JCIE had, simultaneously with its conversations with the Foreign Ministry, been discussing fund-raising with the Keidanren (see Chapter 6). In order to ensure a successful fund-raising campaign, the JCIE enlisted the personal commitment of Mr. Nat-

suaki Fusano, general manager of the Keidanren, who in turn enlisted the support of the president of the Keidanren. The president agreed to sit on the founding committee for the foundation and, together with Mr. Fusano and the JCIE, drafted a list of companies to be approached for contributions.

Although the list was targeted at raising ¥500 million, ¥50 million represented the amount that they felt comfortable about being able to raise as an initial endowment, in advance of any rulings about the extent of tax deductibility. The companies approached for this initial funding were selected solely on the basis of their relationship with the former ambassador.

39. Interview with Mr. Hiroshi Takaku, November 11, 1986.

40. Civil Code, Article 71, Clause 2.

41. "Present Situations and Questions on Non-Profit Public Interest Corporations," Administrative Inspection Bureau of the Management and Coordination Agency (Tokyo: 1984), p. 55ff.

5

Taxation

Tax-exempt status follows automatically from the granting of non-profit status to an organization by the supervising ministry and, as such, is subject to all the discretion inherent in that approval process. The rules that govern the deductibility of contributions, on the other hand, are within the purview of the Finance Ministry and are laid down with greater specificity, though still subject to a great deal of discretion. In this chapter we shall consider the major provisions of the tax law affecting nonprofit organizations, as well as some problems with the current system and proposals for reform.

When we think of nonprofit organizations in the United States, tax considerations come immediately to mind because of the major influence that taxation (or the exemption therefrom) exerts over the life and vitality of these organizations. The tax system both reflects our society's attitude toward nonprofit organizations and, to a great extent, molds their behavior, and the behavior of their donors.

Tax benefits designed for nonprofit enterprises in the United States fall into two main categories, those that affect the organization itself (namely, exemption from tax) and those that affect the donors (namely, reduction of personal tax burdens through the deduction of contributed amounts). The principal exemptions and deductions available to both organizations and individuals are provided through the complex operation of the federal income and estate tax laws.[1] To illustrate the magnitude of the benefit allowed by the federal income tax law, Professor John Simon estimated that in 1985, nonprofit organizations generated approximately $110 billion in fee, sale, and investment revenue that was exempt from income tax. In the same year, he calculated, such organizations received approximately $50 billion in federal tax–deductible contributions.[2]

In Japan as well, the national income tax, with its bifurcated benefits of tax exemption and tax deduction, is the main tax measure affecting private-sector, nonprofit activities. Although taxation generally seems to play a less pivotal role in Japan than in the United States, the exemptions and deductions affecting nonprofit organizations are important and influence the actions of both donors and donees.

Taxation of Nonprofit Organizations

Nonprofit organizations in Japan are exempt from income tax regardless of whether they are formed under the Civil Code, the Trust Law, or any of the various special and generic laws described in Chapter 3. This facet of the tax system, however, is not administered or controlled by the Ministry of Finance. Rather, as indicated in the previous chapter, tax-exempt status automatically follows incorporation as a nonprofit entity and hence is handled by the appropriate competent authority at either the national or the local level. There are more than twenty different branches of the national government alone involved in this process.

The only exception to income tax exemption is that to the extent nonprofit organizations conduct profit-making business activities, as is permitted by law, they must pay income tax on the resulting profits, although they pay at a rate significantly lower than that of the normal corporate income tax. The Finance Ministry has published a list of thirty-three categories of business activities for which nonprofit organizations must pay tax, including publishing, rental of real property, manufacturing, and so on.[3] Business activities not covered by the list may be conducted without any obligation to pay tax. According to the Finance Ministry, the list of taxable enterprises reflects the ministry's judgment that if these particular business functions were allowed to proceed without paying any tax, nonprofit organizations would have an unfair competitive advantage over normal business corporations conducting business in the same field.[4] The fact that all other types of business activities conducted by nonprofit organizations are exempt from tax altogether represents the judgment of the Finance Ministry that such activities are not areas in which taxation affects competitiveness.

For tax and accounting purposes, a nonprofit organization that engages in business must be divided into a profit-making section and a non-profit-making section. The business half is taxed on its profits, and the nonbusiness half is exempt from tax on any income attributable to it (e.g., from membership fees or admission fees). Passive income must be apportioned and allocated to each half. The share attributed to the nonprofit half is tax exempt, whereas that attributed to the business-making half is taxed at normal corporate rates.

Consistent with this bifurcated treatment, the profit-making half of the organization may contribute its profits to the nonprofit half (or to any other nonprofit organization) and receive a deduction against its own income taxes of up to 30 percent of its income for any given tax year. That ceiling goes up to 50 percent of income for contributions to certain educational organizations.

According to Ministry of Finance officials, the rationale behind allowing nonprofit organizations to engage in selected businesses at favorable tax rates is to enable them to support themselves and their activities. In Japan, where fund-raising is neither a well-accepted nor a professionally pursued activity and where most foundations' capital endowments are quite small, this rationale has merit. However, the fact that the profit-making part of the organization may contribute its funds to support its nonprofit half but is not legally required to do so seems somewhat at odds with the ministry's rationale. It also creates an opportunity for tax abuse, as we shall see later in this chapter.

Taxation of Individual Donors

Unlike the granting of tax exemption to nonprofit organizations, the deductibility of contributions by donors is largely controlled by a single government agency, the Ministry of Finance. This is particularly true in the case of individual contributions. As we found in Chapter 2, there is little tradition of individual philanthropy in Japan, a fact reflected in the tax code, which does not allow any income tax deduction for contributions by individuals to nonprofit organizations, except

1. Contributions to the government.
2. Contributions raised from the public at large for donation to a group of organizations specially designated by the Finance Min-

istry as having some extreme national importance (these are called *shitekifukin*, or "designated contributions").
3. Contributions to another category of organizations specially defined by the Finance Ministry as *tokutei kōeki zōshin hōjin*, or "special public-interest–promoting corporations" (referred to hereafter as SPIPCs).[5]

This refers to contributions of cash only; I shall cover contributions of property later in this chapter.

In any of these three cases, contributions over ¥10,000 (at an exchange rate of ¥140/$1, or approximately $70 to $75) in any tax year are deductible up to a limit (for all three categories as a whole) of 25 percent of the donor's income for that year.[6] On the surface, this is a rather generous deduction limit; however, we must first translate the meaning of the items in the preceding list to determine the true scope of the deduction.[7]

Item 1 is fairly self-explanatory. Contributions to the government and its agencies are deductible if they are not made primarily for, and do not result in the receipt of, some special overriding benefit for the donor. An example of a disqualified contribution might be the donation of money to construct a municipal conference or exhibit hall used primarily by the donor and/or managed by the donor for a profit.

Item 2 constitutes a category of contribution called *shitekifukin*, or "designated contribution." Superficially, this provision, too, looks fairly broad, but in practice it represents a rather small range of contributions and a much smaller range than a literal reading of the law itself suggests. Like the public-charities concept in U.S. tax law, *shitekifukin* incorporates the notion that in order to qualify for a tax deduction (or, in the U.S. case, an expanded tax deduction) a contribution must clearly be dedicated to the public interest, and the fact that contributions are collected from the public as a whole, rather than from one or two major sources, is itself an indication that the public interest is being served.

Unlike the U.S. provision, *shitekifukin* further requires that the specific public interest served must be deemed "urgently necessary" by the Ministry of Finance. There are no standards for determining what is "urgently necessary," but in practice, the provision has been used almost entirely for contributions to capital campaigns of a limited duration. Thus, in general, the Ministry of Finance designates an organization as eligible to receive *shitekifukin* for a period of not more than two years and solely for the purpose of raising funds to construct a campus, hospital, library, or similar capital improvement.[8]

Item 3, *tokutei kōeki zōshin hōjin*, refers to nonprofit organizations either mentioned specifically by name or included in any one of a group of categories established in advance by the Ministry of Finance.[9] As a practical matter, most private (as opposed to quasi-public) SPIPCs are organizations involved predominantly in either education or research in the natural and applied sciences. Until the tax law was revised in April, 1988, this special category of nonprofit organization was called *shikenkenkyūhōjin*, or "experimental research corporations" (ERCs). *Shikenkenkyūhōjin*, and the special tax status that attached to them, were created in the 1960s to stimulate private investment in scientific research and education. Consequently, the original ERCs included only scientific research and scholarship organizations. Over time, the scope of ERCs was expanded to encompass eighteen different categories of activities, including the dissemination and enhancement of art and culture and the preservation of cultural assets and the natural environment. Only one category covered international activities of any kind. This category for "economic assistance to developing countries, including technological assistance" was little utilized and seems to have favored technological programs.

After several years of concerted lobbying efforts by Japanese organizations active in international activities, the tax law was amended in April 1988 to add to the list of ERCs a category for organizations promoting "international understanding" of Japan. Because the nomenclature "experimental research organization" was then too narrow, the entire category was renamed "special public-interest-promoting corporation." In August 1988, the JCIE, one of the first foundations in Japan to participate in international activities and one of the prime lobbyists for the change in the tax law, became the first nonprofit organization to receive the new SPIPC status as an organization promoting international understanding.

Despite the continuing liberalization of this special third category of eligible deductions, most of the organizations qualified to receive such deductible contributions still are scientific and educational organizations or quasi-governmental agencies. Presumably this fact represents the continuing government bias in favor of such activities. Taking the example of the new SPIPC category for organizations promoting international understanding of Japan, the JCIE is still the only truly private organization to have attained that privilege. The handful of other recipients have been quasi-governmental organizations, such as the Japan Center for Information and Cultural Affairs (an affiliate of the Foreign Ministry) and the Association for Communication of Transcultural Study (an affiliate of the Ministry of International Trade and Industry).[10]

Private nonprofit organizations wishing to qualify as SPIPCs must apply for that designation to the Finance Ministry — actually the Finance Ministry in conjunction with the relevant competent authority — under one or more of the specially listed categories. These organizations cannot apply to become SPIPCs until after they have received formal nonprofit corporation status from the appropriate ministry.[11] At that time, the Ministry of Finance, in consultation with the supervising ministry, will consider such an application.

Like the incorporation procedure, the process of applying for SPIPC status has few fixed steps or standards and is a time-consuming process of informal *nemawashi*, negotiation, and the submission of documents. To some extent, the negotiations are handled on behalf of the nonprofit organization by the supervising ministry, and so that ministry's support for the tax-favored status can be critical, but ultimately, SPIPC status is granted at the discretion of the Ministry of Finance.

Much as I queried Finance Ministry officials about the criteria important to their SPIPC determination, I was not able to elicit any response more precise than a repetition of the criteria contained in the rather broad statutory language that I quoted earlier. The only specific information I was able to obtain was that the review and approval process for becoming an SPIPC usually takes at least one year from the time the organization begins operations and can take as much as two to three years. This was confirmed by organizations that have undergone the process.[12] Also confirmed by such organizations was the fact that the time period varies according to the importance the government ascribes to the particular organization and the strength of the personal relationships used to bring the organization to the Finance Ministry's attention. Thus, for example, the Ushiba Foundation (discussed in Chapter 4), named for a former ambassador to the United States and strongly backed by powerful members of the Foreign Ministry, received its SPIPC status in under eight months.[13]

SPIPC status is usually granted for a period of two years. The renewal of tax status every two years is essentially a formality, although in theory at least it gives the ministries an opportunity to review and reconsider their decision based on an organization's performance during that period.

Our discussion has dealt solely with individual lifetime contributions of cash. Lifetime contributions of property are treated differently. In general, if an individual makes a lifetime transfer of property, he or she must recognize the gain and pay tax accordingly. This includes transfers of property through donation or contribution. Such transfers are treated as taxable sales of property at fair market value, and no corresponding deduction is available. The only exceptions to this "double-whammy" treatment arise when

1. The gift or bequest of property has been made to the state or a local public body.
2. The gift or bequest is made to a juridical person established in accordance with the provision of Article 34 of the Civil Code and other juristic persons engaged in activities whose purpose is the provision of public facilities . . . , provided that such a gift or bequest is approved by the Minister of Finance as prescribed by cabinet order.[14]

In other words, an individual may make a gift of appreciated property to the state or to a certain limited category of organizations approved by the Ministry of Finance, without having to pay tax on any gain attributable to the appreciation of the property. Still, however, no deduction is allowed.

The range of contributions to which the second exception applies is extremely unclear but also seems extremely narrow. Although the statutory language is similar to the language defining *shitekifukin* contributions of cash, it is not identical and appears even more restricted. Neither private tax accountants nor Finance Ministry officials were able to say definitively whether the overlap between the two provisions is intended to be complete.[15] In any event, unlike contributions of cash, there is no third category giving beneficial treatment to gifts of property to SPIPCs. Like contributions of cash, however, the deductibility of gifts of property is ultimately governed by the discretion of the Ministry of Finance.

The statutory language governing contributions of property refers to both gifts and bequests; thus both lifetime transfers and transfers of property by will or bequest to the appropriate type of organization can be made without recognition of gain. Normally, Japanese tax law imposes inheritance tax on the recipients of an estate who are individuals (rather than an estate tax on the estate itself). The inheritance tax will not apply to individual beneficiaries, however, if the recipient donates the estate to "corporations specified by government ordinance as greatly contributing to the promotion of education or science, enhancement of culture, social welfare, or other public-interest juristic persons."[16]

Once again the scope of this exception depends on the ministry's discretion, and it is not clear whether this language is intended to duplicate the statutory language applicable to contributions of cash by individuals during their lifetimes or is intended to be read more narrowly. The mere fact that there is no answer to these questions is one sure indication that the provisions applicable to donations by individuals are infrequently and insignificantly used.

In a chicken-and-egg way, the limited scope of the deductions available to individuals both reflects and perpetuates the low importance currently attached to individual philanthropic activity in Japan. As discussed in Chapter 2, culture and tradition militate against this type of individual initiative, favoring instead collective group action. That bias is reflected in the more liberal tax incentives offered to corporate donors.

Taxation of Corporate Donors

The income tax deduction available to corporate donors to nonprofit organizations is more liberal than that allowed to individual contributors. Corporations receive an income tax deduction for contributions to all nonprofit organizations and receive an expanded deduction for certain types of contributions.

For tax purposes, corporate contributions are divided into four categories:

1. Contributions to the government or its agencies.
2. *Shitekifukin*, or "designated contributions."
3. Contributions to SPIPCs.
4. "General contributions" to all Civil Code and other nonprofit organizations, including religious and political societies.[17]

The first three categories are virtually identical to the three categories of contributions that are deductible for individuals. However, the limitations on deductibility for all three types of contribution are much higher for corporations than for individuals. Corporations may deduct, without limit, 100 percent of any contributions to the government or "designated" contributions (Categories 1 and 2). In addition, corporations may deduct the amount of their contributions to SPIPCs up to a limit equal to 1/2 × (0.0025 × capital + 0.025 × income). Finally, in addition to the deductions available on the first three categories, corporations may deduct general contributions (Category 4) up to an amount equal to 1/2 × (0.0025 × capital + 0.025 × income). In other words, the limit that applies to contributions to SPIPCs applies again, and separately, to general contributions.

This last category, "general contributions," marks the greatest distinction between the benefits available to corporations and those available to individuals. Remarkably, however, most of the people I interviewed were totally unaware of the availability of this category of deduction. In one case, I had quite a vehement argument with a gentleman, himself helping establish a corporate foundation, who insisted that no such "general" category existed. After checking with his contacts in the Finance Ministry, he conceded that I was, in fact, correct. The pervasive gap in knowledge among experts about the existence of this provision can, I believe, be attributed to the fact that in most cases, corporate donors use up their "general contributions" limitation through contributions to politicians and political organizations. They therefore view this as a tax deduction for political contributions and are not even aware that the category includes a much wider range of "charitable" activities.

The provisions governing corporate contributions of appreciated property are also more generous than those applicable to individuals. Upon the transfer of property to any nonprofit organization, the donor corporation is deemed to have sold the property for an amount equal to its fair market value at the time of transfer and then to have donated the cash proceeds from the sale. Thus the corporation pays a tax on the deemed income[18] but receives a corresponding deduction, limited in accordance with the preceding four categories of contributions.[19]

Similarly, when a corporation sells property to a nonprofit organization for a price lower than fair market value (bargain sale), the property is deemed to have been sold for its fair value and is taxed accordingly. The "bargain" element (the difference between fair market value and the actual sales proceeds) is deemed to be a contribution and is deductible in accordance with the preceding rules.

In the case of corporations, the law broadly defines contributions to include transactions with any person in which a corporation grants any kind of economic benefit without receiving reasonable consideration. Thus, at least in theory, the provision of facilities or equipment free of charge or at a bargain rate constitutes a tax-deductible contribution to the extent of the excess of benefit transferred over the consideration received. A similarly broad definition of the term *contributions* does not appear to apply to individuals.

International Contributions — Supplementary Mechanism

The preceding discussion has set forth the major legal provisions governing the taxation of nonprofit organizations and their donors, both individual and corporate. In addition to the specific statutory rules, a supplementary mechanism has been developed to facilitate contributions by Japanese donors (particularly corporate donors) to overseas organizations.

All of the tax provisions detailed thus far in this chapter apply to Japanese nonprofit organizations and donations to such organiza-

tions alone. Donations to nonprofit organizations or activities overseas are not tax deductible, with one major exception[20] (see also the
discussion in Chapter 7 of the MITI proposal regarding the creation
of another flow-through organization). Upon application and approval, the Japan Foundation — a quasi-governmental organization
under the supervision of the Foreign Ministry — acts as a middleman, funneling contributions to overseas organizations of the corporations' choosing. Because the Japan Foundation itself is an
SPIPC, contributions to it are tax deductible within the limits prescribed by law for corporations and individuals.

The Japan Foundation was established by special legislation in
1972 under the aegis of the Foreign Ministry, for the purpose of
promoting an understanding of Japanese culture abroad. The original intention of the Foreign Ministry was to create a ¥100 billion
endowment fund of which the government would contribute half
and private businesses would contribute half. To date, the government has contributed its share to the foundation's endowment, but
the private sector has contributed less than 10 percent of its allotted
endowment amount. It is perhaps for this reason that the mechanism developed of allowing private sources to contribute through
the Japan Foundation rather than to the Japan Foundation. The
flow-through structure has the advantage of allowing the donor to
designate the target for its contribution and to attach its name to
the funds (thereby receiving any resulting accolades and publicity),
whereas a contribution to the foundation's general endowment fund
may carry the donor's name but does not allow the donor to direct
the disbursement of its funds.

The mechanics for making a grant through the Japan Foundation
are relatively straightforward, and although the process relies heavily on the discretion of the Japan Foundation and the Foreign Ministry, it is much more clearly defined and presented than are the
general processes required to establish a foundation or obtain designation as an SPIPC. After testing the water through the now-
familiar process of *nemawashi*, the first step is for a potential donor
or group of donors to submit an application to the Japan Foundation setting forth the amount of the proposed donation, the name
of the overseas organization for which the donation is intended, the
activities for which the money will be used, and a description of the
circumstances leading to the offer of donation. In order to be ac-

cepted, the proposed project must fall within the scope of valid Japan Foundation activities and accordingly must be one that contributes to cultural exchange, in the following specific areas: Japanese studies and Japanese-language education at foreign educational and research institutions, kabuki performances, Japanese art galleries in foreign museums, and the construction and improvement of related facilities.[21]

Eligible grantees are limited to overseas nonprofit organizations of high and acknowledged repute, such as major universities and research institutes or organizations similarly oriented toward the "public interest." Once an application has been reviewed and approved by the Japan Foundation and the money has actually been transferred to the foundation, the project is submitted for the final approval of the Ministry of Foreign Affairs.[22]

The Japan Foundation's flow-through mechanism has been well utilized: Virtually all the large Japanese corporate grants to museums, research institutes, and universities in the United States have been made in this way. In fact, during the period from the founding of the Japan Foundation to the end of its 1988 fiscal year, ¥29 billion (approximately $207 million, at an exchange rate of ¥140/$1) was donated to international causes through specified donations to the Japan Foundation.[23]

Despite its benefits in converting otherwise nondeductible contributions overseas into deductible ones, the flow-through system has its drawbacks. Because the mandate of the Japan Foundation itself is limited to intercultural programs that somehow promote an understanding of Japan, contributions made through the Japan Foundation are limited in the same manner. In addition, although individuals are entitled to use the Japan Foundation's mechanism, as a practical matter the device has been used almost exclusively for funneling large corporate grants. Individuals have been permitted to use the system only in conjunction with a larger corporate fundraising program.

The system has not been used, and is unlikely to be used, for small individual contributions or for grants to small organizations, particularly because the Japan Foundation rules specifically state that the recipient must be an organization deemed reliable and prestigious by the foundation and the Foreign Ministry. Finally, the Japan Foundation is essentially a government foundation, and its grants are, accordingly, subject to government influence and approval, once again blending the boundaries between private philanthropic activity and government policy.

Problems with the Tax System

The major and consistent complaint voiced about taxation of the nonprofit sector in Japan is that the tax system is too miserly, that laws ought to be liberalized to provide more generous tax benefits to both organizations and donors. (We shall examine some of the proposals advanced for tax reform in the next section of this chapter.) Difficulties with the tax system, however, are not confined to the letter of the law itself but, rather, encompass the way in which the law is interpreted, implemented, and administered.

Perhaps the major problem, and one alluded to previously, is the decentralization of authority for granting tax benefits to nonprofit organizations. The two main benefits provided by Japanese law to the nonprofit sector are the tax-exempt status of organizations and the deductibility of contributions by donors; yet the granting of these benefits is not handled entirely by the Ministry of Finance, which is otherwise responsible for overseeing and administering the tax code. Rather, the exemption of organizations from tax stems automatically from the granting of their nonprofit status by the appropriate authorizing ministry; and the availability of tax deductions to donors, though much more tightly and directly supervised by the Ministry of Finance (through its ability to define SPIPCs and designated contributions) is not entirely within its purview either.[24]

With respect to the granting of tax exemption, there is no legal requirement that the authorizing ministries inform the Finance Ministry (or, where relevant, the local branch of the NTA) of the grant of nonprofit status to an organization. In the absence of any such requirement, it seems that these ministries do not in fact routinely notify the Finance Ministry, as neither NTA nor other Finance Ministry officials were able to supply accurate statistics for the total number of tax-exempt organizations nationwide.[25] This is particularly problematic with respect to the granting of tax-exempt status by local government agencies.

If not actually informed by a supervising agency, the Ministry of Finance has no formal means of learning about or keeping track of tax-exempt nonprofit organizations, as the organizations are not required to file annual information or tax returns with the Ministry of Finance, except to the extent that they are engaged in a taxable, profit-making activity. All nonprofit organizations, of course, must submit annual program and financial reports to the supervising ministry, but these are not routinely transmitted to the Ministry of Finance. By contrast, in the United States, all nonprofit organizations are required to file an annual information return with the IRS in lieu of the tax return required of profit-making entities.

The only situations in which Ministry of Finance is likely to receive formal information about a nonprofit organization is if the organization conducts profit-making businesses, is an SPIPC, or is eligible to receive designated contributions. In the first case, the organization is required to file a tax return similar to that filed by any other business.[26] In the other two cases, the Finance Ministry usually participates in granting such special tax status and is empowered to review that status every two years; hence its information is fairly complete and up-to-date.

The decentralization of authority over nonprofit tax matters complicates the task of policing these organizations and has fostered a rather lax adherence by many nonprofit organizations to taxation principles. A 1985 National Tax Administration (NTA) survey of approximately one thousand nonprofit organizations revealed that approximately 91 percent of these organizations failed to report part or all of their income from profitable business activities, resulting in a loss of tax revenue to the government of ¥13.3 billion ($95 million), or ¥13 million per organization in fiscal 1985. The average undeclared income per organization was ¥13 million ($91,000), more than two times the average undeclared income for normal business corporations in the same year.[27] In addition, an estimated 76 percent of such corporations failed to collect, withhold, and remit taxes, as required, from their employees' incomes.[28]

As the statistics suggest, a problem related to, and perhaps exacerbated by, the decentralized supervision of the nonprofit system is the officially sanctioned bifurcation of exempt organizations into nonprofit and for-profit segments and the corresponding tax benefits accorded to the for-profit half. It is not the rationale for the dual system that is at fault but, rather, its execution.

Although the two halves of the nonprofit organization are supposed to be accounted for and taxed separately, with the profit-half paying tax on its profits as well as on passive income attributable to its investments, the NTA investigation indicates that these rules are honored largely in the breach. For the most part, the income undeclared by nonprofit organizations in 1985 was hidden by a shifting of income and expenses between the nonprofit organizations' two halves: Revenues from profit-seeking business were reported as nonprofit revenue, and expenses incurred in connection with nonprofit activities were reported as business expenses.[29]

The fact that the per-capita tax evasion in the nonprofit sector exceeded that in the private-business sector in 1985 suggests that at least some of these nonprofit organizations are being formed and/ or utilized specifically to reduce taxes. Of course, nonprofit organizations do not have shareholders, and accordingly, the profits from their business activities cannot be distributed as dividends. Nonetheless, because there is no requirement that profits be plowed back into nonprofit activities, they can, in theory, be taken out in the form of excessive salaries, expense accounts, or other benefits.[30] Alternatively, they can be reinvested in the organization's profit-making business. (Even if no direct monetary benefit is taken out, the availability of tax-free funds for reinvestment may allow the business to operate at effectively lower costs and hence at a competitive advantage relative to normal corporations.) These are precisely the types of risks and abuses to which the dormant foundations lend themselves. The magnitude of tax abuse uncovered by the NTA 1985 survey suggests that there are in fact many more foundations being used primarily for tax advantage—and hence are dormant in the general sense of nonperformance of their stated function—than the officially defined and identified number of 572 (see the discussion of dormant foundations in Chapter 4).

Income tax evasion schemes are further aided by the fact that neither the Japanese tax code nor any other law relating to nonprofit organizations contains specific regulatory laws, comparable to the IRS rules governing U.S. private foundations, to deter and penalize this type of behavior. I shall briefly review the background and major provisions of the private foundation rules adopted by the IRS in 1969, in order to understand how and where abuses of the system may take place.

During the prosperous 1950s, the number of private foundations in the United States and the scope of their activities increased perceptibly. For the first time, the general public became aware of, and began to feel somewhat uneasy about, foundation activities, not being sure exactly what these entities represented. In the early 1960s, at the urging of Congressman Wright Patman, the Treasury Department launched an investigation of private foundation dealings, specifically financial dealings, and found what they believed to be a number of violations of the spirit, if not the letter, of the law.[31] Based on these findings, continuing pressure by Congressman Patman, and a general perception of foundations as impenetrable and secretive bastions of wealth and power, a new study was undertaken by the House Ways and Means Committee in 1969. The result of this study was the adoption of a number of measures tightening the regulatory environment for private foundations.[32]

These new restrictive measures included: (1) an excise tax on investment income to cover the cost of IRS expenses associated with policing foundations (IRC, Section 4940); (2) "self-dealing" rules prohibiting certain kinds of transactions (e.g., rental or sale of goods, services, facilities; loans of money) between foundations and their fiduciaries or donors (IRC, Section 4941); (3) a minimum "payout" rule requiring foundations to make annual distributions equal to the greater of 5 percent of foundation assets or all income, later changed to a payout based on 5 percent of assets only (IRC, Section 4942); (4) a limit on the amount of stock that a foundation and its fiduciaries or donors can own in a business ("excess business holdings" rule, IRC, Section 4943); (5) a tax on investments that jeopardize or are deemed risky to the foundation's ability to maintain its assets and carry out its charitable purpose (IRC, Section 4944); and (6) a tax aimed at prohibiting or regulating foundation grants to individuals, other foundations, nonexempt organizations, or political campaigns (IRC, Section 4945). In addition, in conformity with these changes, the information required of private foundations on their annual information returns (Form 990) was expanded, and foundations were required to make this information available to the general public and to file these returns with the states in which they were incorporated.

Ministry of Finance officials with whom I talked felt that tax abuse was not a major concern with respect to nonprofit organizations, yet the NTA's own findings about the extent of unreported business income alone suggest that perhaps it should be. In addition, the public perception seems to diverge somewhat from the Finance Ministry's point of view. Finally, my own research yielded several cases of what in the United States prompted the adoption of the self-dealing and excess business holdings rules and today would be violations of those rules. In particular, the practice among wealthy, family-controlled corporations of transferring significantly appreciated and often controlling blocks of stock to a corporate-established and -controlled foundation was not uncommon. Because the foundations are not required to divest the stock and the corporation and foundation often have overlapping boards of directors, the transfer enables the corporation to continue its business activities unchanged and enables the corporate and/or individual donors to protect their controlling interests in the company and yet to receive a significant tax deduction for the "donation" of stock.

The existence of and potential for tax abuse are exacerbated by the fact that the "competent authorities" primarily responsible for granting tax-exempt status and verifying its continued validity are not taxation specialists. They are the various ministries of the government, other than the Ministry of Finance. Quite understandably, their interests and expertise do not lie in parsing the tax code and enforcing its dictates. Even within the Ministry of Finance and the NTA, no single division focuses on issues involving exempt organizations. Perhaps this lack of focus helps explain why the Ministry of Finance officials I queried intimated that tax abuse in the nonprofit sector was not a major concern. To date, I am aware of no comprehensive review of the tax and regulatory environment governing nonprofit organizations that would be comparable to the review undertaken by the U.S. IRS in 1969, and yet in terms of perceptions and problems, Japanese foundations may have reached a similar stage.

If the absence of a central clearinghouse for tax matters creates oversight difficulties for the government, on the flip side it creates an information gap for organizations seeking to understand how the system works. Without full and clear information they are unable to take advantage of the benefits validly available. By way of illustration: Mr. Toshio Hara, the well-informed and energetic founder and chairman of the Hara Museum of Contemporary Art in Tokyo, was unaware that one of the SPIPC categories includes arts organizations, having been told that SPIPC status was available only for scientific and educational programs; advisers to a fledgling organization trying to establish a foundation in Japan did not know that such a thing as a SPIPC existed at all; and a former government official seeking contributions for a soon-to-be-established foundation believed that the only tax-deductible corporate contributions were those to SPIPCs.[33]

Another area of difficulty with the tax system is the categorization of organizations as "general" nonprofit organizations, SPIPCs, organizations eligible to receive *shitekifukin* or "designated contributions," and the resulting differentiation among types and deductibility of contributions. The categorization of organizations itself is not a problem.[34] What is troublesome is that the standards for positioning organizations in the hierarchy are not systematized, and because they rely so heavily on government discretion, they continue to be rather arbitrary and to reflect government rather than private preferences.

The whole concept of SPIPCs was developed initially by the government as a means of encouraging private-sector support for urgently needed scientific and technological advancement during the postwar era, and the system continues to reflect that early bias.[35] Although exact figures are not available, it seems that of those SPIPCs whose status is not granted by special legislation, science and science-related organizations account for approximately 40 percent, with educational and scholarship organizations reflecting another 35 to 40 percent.[36] The clear preference in the tax code for scientific and scholarship programs accomplishes what it was intended to; namely, it encourages private support for these activities, yet it correspondingly fails to encourage the growth of a broader range of social, cultural, or international activities. As of 1987, fewer than 10 percent of SPIPCs were engaged in the arts or in international activities.[37] Among Japanese nonprofit organizations engaged in

the latter fields of endeavor, this was the most widely and vehement-
ly criticized aspect of the nonprofit system.

A final and particularly disturbing area of the tax law is the
definition of corporate "general" contributions, those other than
designated contributions or contributions to SPIPCs. As we pointed out earlier, this general category includes political contributions
to parties, individuals, causes, and candidates. Because political
contributions and other general charitable contributions are indistinguishable in their treatment under the tax law, it is nearly
impossible to get an accurate sense of the true magnitude of corporate contributions to philanthropic—as opposed to political—
causes.

The statistics widely cited as representing annual corporate charitable giving are culled by the NTA from corporate tax returns. On
the corporate tax return, designated contributions (*shitekifukin*)
and contributions to SPIPCs are separately reported, but all general
contributions are lumped together. Thus, because both political and
charitable contributions are part of the general category, it is not
possible to determine the exact breakdown between the two. Off the
record, one Ministry of Finance official indicated to me that probably the bulk of contributions in the general category were in fact
political contributions.

According to NTA statistics, in 1985, general contributions accounted for about 65 percent of total corporate contributions. In
1986, general contributions accounted for 67 percent (¥204.9 billion) of the total, and designated contributions and contributions to
SPIPCs accounted for approximately 20 percent (¥60.4 billion) and
13 percent (¥41.4 billion), respectively.[38] For the same year, the
Home Affairs Ministry reported that Japanese politicians and political organizations collected ¥167.59 billion in political donations.[39]
Of course, these donations came from civic groups, labor organizations, and individuals as well as from companies; nonetheless, the
apparent correlation between this number and the number cited by
the NTA as representing corporate "general contributions" would
seem to suggest that most of these general contributions are in fact
dedicated to political causes.

The combining of the two types of donation under a single deduction limitation clearly restricts the amount that corporations are
willing to give to nonpolitical, charitable organizations that fall in

the general category. Unfortunately, the majority of Japanese non-profit organizations fall into this category. In addition, this combining seems to have distorted the corporations' own understanding of the deductibility of various types of contributions. Many fundraisers, both American and Japanese, said that in the course of their fund-raising efforts they were told by Japanese corporations that the corporation would be entitled to a tax deduction only if it contributed to an SPIPC. This is not an accurate interpretation of the law but may reflect the fact that many corporations use up and even exceed their general contributions limitation by making political contributions; thus as a practical matter, any additional donations would not be deductible (unless given to a designated organization, an SPIPC, or the government).

A few years ago, this overlapping of political and philanthropic giving was barely acknowledged, much less widely discussed. Many whom I confronted with the question flatly denied that political contributions were included in the general contribution category. I was particularly intrigued to find that the Keidanren, which plays such a pivotal role in both political and charitable fund-raising, did not seem aware (or else was reluctant to admit) that the figures it routinely cites as representing corporate "charitable" contributions include political donations as well.

The Recruit Cosmos political scandals of 1989 seem to have brought into the open this issue, as part of the overall political maelstrom. Although it remains far from a major concern for most, it is at least now recognized and may receive some attention as the whole system of political contributions and influence buying comes under review in the Japanese Diet.

Although I believe the blending of political and charitable contributions has been largely detrimental to the cause of philanthropy, the failure to distinguish between the two types of giving should, perhaps, not be surprising in a country where traditionally so much deference has been given to government. If the "public interest" and the "government interest" are synonymous in people's minds, why distinguish between them in the tax law? This is in marked contrast with the United States where public and government interest have not always been deemed to coincide and where political and charitable contributions are not only separately treated but political contributions are also rather strictly circumscribed.

Tax System Reform

Japanese who work in the nonprofit area are certainly not unaware of the problems inherent in the existing tax system, its failure both to provide sufficiently generous tax incentives and to provide adequate safeguards against the abuse of existing tax benefits. Scholars in this field have given considerable attention to possible tax reforms. Since 1975, Dr. Minoru Tanaka, professor of law, Keio University, and Ms. Takako Amemiya, assistant professor, Shoin Women's College, and specialist, Japan Association of Charitable Corporations, have consistently analyzed routes for improving the current system. The Japan Center for International Exchange, spearheaded by Mr. Tadashi Yamamoto, has sponsored numerous conferences and study missions that have included tax issues on their agendas.

In addition, in the summer of 1983, under the joint auspices of the Suntory Foundation and the Nippon Life Insurance Foundation, a group of scholars and foundation personnel were sent on a study mission to the United States to collect information on the U.S. legal (and, in particular, tax) system governing nonprofit organizations. Their findings have been published, and their recommendations for tax reform have been submitted to the Japanese government.[40]

Almost all of the reform proposals propounded to date contain recommendations based on the U.S. system of taxing nonprofit organizations (e.g., increase the deduction limit for corporations, give individuals a deduction similar to that in the United States, and raise the allowable deduction for contributions of appreciated property), and although these have merit, they should be approached with some caution. Before adopting, wholesale, various aspects of the U.S. tax system, it seems worth asking why the United States has developed such a system, whether it works, and whether or not a comparable system makes sense in Japan, given the overall legal and social structure of which the nonprofit system is merely a part.

As a result of its own peculiar history and culture, the United States is uniquely reliant on private funding for philanthropic activities and on tax incentives to encourage such activities. From the beginning, the diversity of Americans and the rate of growth of the American states defied the ability of government to keep up. Consequently, Americans felt it necessary to form diverse, self-governing, and self-sufficient community units, for which they still retain a preference. Indeed, that preference is reflected in the federal government system and, to some measure, in the tax code.

Although many European countries also provide tax benefits, none has so extensive a system as the United States does, because they rely—and prefer to rely—more heavily on direct government funding and provision of services.[41] In this respect, Japan is much closer to a European model. It has an extremely powerful central government that people expect to attend to their needs and desires. In a small, relatively homogeneous country this type of centralized system makes some sense. As Japan becomes more internationalized and internally more diverse, some feel that the benefits of such a powerful central government may wane. Nonetheless, Japan might benefit from and should at least consider European models of philanthropy before adopting U.S. blueprints.

In both Japan and the United States, arguments supporting liberalization (or, in the United States, maintenance) of tax benefits for donors to nonprofit organizations assume that there is a direct correlation between the tax benefit available and the giving that takes place. Even in the United States, with its long tradition of reliance on tax incentives, such a proposition has been difficult to prove. At best, the numerous studies of the price elasticity of charitable giving seem to indicate that although the amounts that donors are willing to give may vary in conjunction with the "cost" of such giving, the determination of whether to give does not. It is even less clear in Japan, where the culture itself has not traditionally supported private philanthropy, that either the motivation to give or the magnitude of giving would increase significantly with the availability of greater tax benefits.

Even at this point in Japan, opinions about the importance of tax incentives are divided. Mr. Mikio Kato of International House indicated that in his fund-raising campaigns, corporation rarely exhibit concern about the deductibility of their contributions. Instead they inquire about what they will receive in return for their donations and whether their business competitors and colleagues have contributed.[42] This view was echoed by several American fund-raisers who were surprised that in the course of their solicitations, the issue of deductibility was never raised. But others held a diametrically opposed view, saying that they were unable to elicit funding commitments from corporations without an assurance that the contributions would be deductible. Mr. Natsuaki Fusano, general manager, Keidanren, stated that the Keidanren rarely extends fund-raising assistance to an organization that is not an SPIPC or otherwise eligible to receive deductible contributions.[43]

The uncertainty as to the impact of tax liberalization on giving patterns is, I believe, particularly pronounced with respect to individual giving, an area in which liberalization has been enthusiastically advanced. In the United States, tax deductibility is only one of a host of factors—and not the most important one—inspiring individuals to give. According to a study published by the Independent Sector in 1986, the individuals who are most generous in their charitable giving share the following characteristics:

1. They attend religious services regularly.
2. They perceive that they have a moderate amount or a lot of discretionary income.
3. They have no worries about having enough money in the future.
4. They volunteer their time in philanthropic activities.
5. They worry little or only moderately about money.[44]

As we noted in Chapter 2, most Japanese do worry about money and do not perceive themselves as having a great deal of disposable income. Moreover, they do not regularly attend religious services, in the Western sense, and do not volunteer their time. Of course, given the cultural differences between Japan and the United States, the factors that will motivate charitable behavior in Japanese individuals are likely to differ from those that motivate Americans, but there is no reason to think that Japanese individuals will be more motivated by tax concerns than their American counterparts will. In fact, they are likely to be less influenced by taxes—at least at present—for the following reasons.

In addition to cultural and philosophical considerations, any proposals for tax reform in the nonprofit area must also be viewed practically, in the context of the overall tax system. It is all too easy for U.S. and Japanese scholars to look at the nonprofit area and to say that changes should be made, but such changes are never made in isolation. They inevitably affect other areas of the tax law with no apparent connection to the nonprofit area. A few examples: Some people feel that in Japan both companies and individuals focus less on tax planning than do their typical American counterparts. At least with respect to individuals, there are some practical reasons that this might be so. First, in Japan most individuals do not file an income tax return (or file only an abbreviated "short form" return); rather, income tax is automatically withheld from their salaries by their employers. As a result, many people just do not think about tax issues. Furthermore, if an individual were to make a charitable contribution, he or she would have to file a separate, special income tax return, thereby incurring additional paperwork and the possibility of increased scrutiny by tax authorities.

Second, the people who worry about tax planning anywhere are generally people with money. The amassment of huge individual fortunes in Japan is a relatively new phenomenon, and despite its dramatic proportions, it is not yet widely or openly acknowledged. Most Japanese regard themselves and their country as solidly middle class (see Chapter 2). Although this may be consistent with their general desire to be part of a group of like individuals, it is no longer quite coincident with reality. Nonetheless, it influences their attitudes toward charitable giving and toward the tax code as a tool of giving.

One gentleman with whom I had a lively discussion about the possible direction of tax reform in the nonprofit area vigorously and vociferously proclaimed that the incentives for individual giving in the U.S. tax code were designed to, and in fact do, benefit the rich only and that Japanese would never tolerate such an inegalitarian system. Although his view was rather extremely phrased and presented, it contains the nugget of truth that the Japanese do not yet see themselves as wealthy people and, as individuals, do not want to distinguish themselves from the crowd on the basis of wealth.

More concretely, the Japanese legal system does not, at this point, provide governing regulations comparable to the U.S. private foundation rules to deter abuses of the tax system. Because opportunities for abuse often go hand in hand with liberalization, several reform proposals have advanced inclusion of these types of regulations. Again, this cannot be viewed in isolation. Such rules would undoubtedly have a salutary effect, but this effect could be diminished by the fact that the Japanese tax administration system is not computerized in a way that allows for the cross-checking and validation of information.[45]

Japanese taxpayers — whether individual or corporate — do not have a social security number or any other equivalent taxpayer ID number. Without ID numbers, computerized auditing and cross-checking of information — for example, confirmation that amounts claimed as deductions by one source are reported as income or contributions by another — is impossible, and in a country of 120 million people tax compliance is ephemeral if not impossible to enforce without computerized auditing. This makes the introduction of any tax liberalization worthy of serious advance consideration.[46]

My remarks are not offered with any intent to discredit or discourage existing or future proposals for reform of the tax system as it relates to nonprofit organizations. Rather, they are intended to encourage efforts based on a broad understanding of the overall tax, legal, and cultural environment and to caution restraint against the hasty importation and adoption of a system born of different surroundings.

Notes

1. In addition to the significant benefits provided by the federal income tax law, most states follow the federal government in allowing nonprofit organizations to claim exemption from income tax and allowing donors to deduct contributions from their income tax. Perhaps more importantly, state and local governments generally exempt nonprofit organizations from property tax. Professor John Simon estimated that in 1985, nonprofit organizations held an estimated $300 billion in real estate exempt from state and local property taxes. John G. Simon, "The Tax Treatment of Nonprofit Organizations: A Review of Federal and State Policies," in Walter W. Powell, ed., *The Nonprofit Sector: A Research Handbook* (New Haven, Conn.: Yale University Press, 1987), p. 67.

In Japan, as in the United States, the property or asset tax system is a local one and is therefore difficult to describe in general terms. It is a complex tax that may consist of three or more components, including a fixed-assets tax, a special property-holding tax, and a real property acquisition tax (imposed on the purchaser of the property). Unlike the

United States, however, most private nonprofit organizations are not exempt from property taxes. (Religious organizations and quasi-public nonprofit organizations are often exceptions). Because the property tax exemption does not apply to most private nonprofit organizations in Japan, I shall not discuss it. Nonetheless, note that although the property tax is regarded as a critical benefit to many nonprofit organizations in the United States, the lack of property tax benefits does not seem to be of major concern to most Japanese nonprofit organizations today. This is partly because most nonprofit organizations in Japan have a very small asset base relative to their U.S. counterparts. In particular, most corporate foundations receive annual contributions from their corporate sponsors, and so they are not dependent on asset-generated revenues. Arguably, however, the property tax issue is rather a circular one, in that Japanese nonprofit organizations might amass greater assets (with which to generate self-supporting income) if they could be confident that they would not be taxed on such holdings.

2. Simon, "The Tax Treatment of Nonprofit Organizations," p. 67.

3. The complete list includes (1) selling goods, (2) renting real estate, (3) lending money, (4) renting goods, (5) selling real estate, (6) manufacturing, (7) communication business, (8) transportation business, (9) warehousing, (10) contracting, (11) printing, (12) publishing, (13) photographing, (14) seat rental business, (15) hotel business, (16) restaurant and other eating establishments, (17) brokerage business, (18) agency business, (19) mediation, (20) wholesale business, (21) mining, (22) soil collection and stone [quarrying], (23) public bathhouse operation, (24) barber shops, (25) beauty parlors, (26) promotion, (27) recreation hall business, (28) sightseeing business, (29) medical care business, (30) teaching arts, (31) parking business, (32) credit security business, and (33) intangible property [patents]. Article 5, Clause 1, Enforcement Ordinance of the Corporate Tax Law.

According to a 1985 survey by the Management and Coordination Agency, the most popular business activities for nonprofit organizations are publishing, contracting, sale of goods, rental of real estate, medical care, and hotel operation. Management and Coordination Agency survey as cited in Amemiya, "Present Situation and Problems," p. 231.

4. Interview with Mr. Toshio Tojima, manager, Corporate Tax Section, National Tax Administration, November 7, 1986.

This is similar to the rationale that led to the adoption in the United States in 1950 of the "unrelated business tax" provisions of IRC Section 511 ff., taxing the income earned by nonprofit organizations from businesses unrelated to their charitable function. This rationale has been challenged by scholars and economists, some of whom feel that income taxes are not a factor of production that enter into price setting. See, Simon, "The Tax Treatment of Nonprofit Organizations," p. 92.

The whole question of taxing unrelated business profits continues to be controversial in the United States, particularly during the past decade as government services have declined (leaving a larger gap to be filled by nonprofit organizations) and direct government grants to nonprofit organizations have shrunk. Some think the tax should be done away with altogether because of insufficient evidence that income tax actually affects competitiveness, and others argue that an organization should not only be taxed on such profits but also should have its nonprofit status revoked if it engages in too much "commercial" activity.

5. The actual language of the statute is as follows:

1. The endowment is donated to the state or a local public body (provided that the donor does not derive exclusive use from facilities established with his endowment and does not otherwise recognize special profit or benefit from the endowment).

2. The endowment is donated to a juristic person incorporated in accordance with the provisions of Article 34 of the Civil Code or to any other corporation or group performing activities related to the public interest, provided that such organizations have been designated by the Minister of Finance as satisfying the following criteria:
   a. that the endowment is widely collected from the general public.
   b. that the endowment is appropriated to the promotion of education or science, elevation of culture, dedication to social welfare, and other disbursement for increasing public interests that are urgently necessary.

3. The endowment is donated to a corporation listed in item 1 of the attached List no. 1 [SPIPCs] and other corporations incorporated by specific laws, which remarkably contribute to the promotion of education or science, elevation of culture, social welfare, and furtherance of other public interests, as prescribed by cabinet order. . . .

6. The term *income* as it is used here is essentially taxable income, that is, income from which most other deductions have already been subtracted.

7. The deduction limit for individuals in the United States is 30 percent of adjusted gross income for contributions to private foundations and 50 percent of adjusted gross income for contributions to public charities and certain operating foundations. "Adjusted gross income" is basically gross income minus the standard deduction allowed by law. Accordingly, it is a more generous income measurement than "taxable income" is.

8. This provision is also apparently sometimes used for the initial capital endowment of a private foundation. The foundation seeks a temporary ruling from the Ministry of Finance that during the one or two years of its endowment campaign, contributions will be deemed to be *shitekifukin*.

9. The organizations mentioned specifically by name are generally those types of organizations (discussed in Chapter 3) that have been formed by specifically targeted legislation. In addition, many corporations created by generic legislation are also entitled to SPIPC status. Some of these, such as social welfare organizations formed pursuant to the Social Welfare Act, are automatically given such status, without any need for Ministry of Finance approval, which explains why most SPIPCs (about 11,000 out of 12,750) are social welfare organizations. Others, such as schools formed under the Private School Act, are not automatically given tax-favored status but are entitled by law to apply for SPIPC status. As of the end of March 1987, 220 of the total 6,000 schools established under the Private School Act had applied for and received SPIPC status. According to Finance Ministry officials, if an application is filed by such an organization, the grant is virtually assured.

10. According to Mr. Tadashi Yamamoto, the process through which the JCIE was finally awarded SPIPC status made it clear that unless a private organization has a substantial track record behind it, SPIPC status will be extremely difficult to obtain. "This means, ironically, that unless a private organization is sufficiently developed, it is not qualified to receive the tax privilege; therefore potential donors have no tax incentives for helping new independent institutions struggling to establish themselves." Yamamoto and Amenomori, "Japanese Private Philanthropy in an Interdependent World," p. 22.

11. An organization that knows that it wants SPIPC status will begin lobbying and talking informally from the moment it starts the incorporation process.

12. Unfortunately, the timing of receipt of such favored tax status can be critical. Because organizations often need a fairly large capital contribution to become established, they have to solicit donors, but these sources often want to know in advance of making their gift whether it will be deductible, a Catch-22 situation. This problem is of less concern to the majority of foundations established by a single corporate sponsor than it is to those more independent foundations that have to solicit support from a broader group.

13. Interministry politicking may also have an influence on the outcome and timing of an SPIPC application. In some cases, the sponsoring ministry may be very much in favor of granting a tax benefit to an organization under its jurisdiction whereas the Ministry of Finance may be loath to

forgo tax revenue on behalf of an organization that is not directly under its supervision.

14. Special Tax Measures Law, Article 40, Clause 1; and Enforcement Ordinance, Article 25, Clause 9.

15. It also seems that although the language of the law grants the right to make such "tax-free" gifts of property, as a practical matter such gifts by individuals are likely to be audited and reviewed by the NTA. Most individuals in Japan do not file income tax returns on their own (or they file simplified "short" forms), as their entire tax liability is usually satisfied by withholding by their employers. But any individual making a charitable contribution does have to file a return, thus dramatically increasing the likelihood of audit.

16. Special Tax Measures Law, Article 70, Clause 2; Enforcement Ordinance, Article 40.

Because the inheritance tax is imposed only on individuals, no tax is imposed when a nonprofit organization receives donations directly by bequest, with two exceptions. First, if in connection with a bequest to a nonprofit organization (or other similar organization), the nonprofit organization grants "special benefits to its founder, member, director, supervisor, person who made a gift or bequest to the said corporation, their relative or others who are in a special relationship therewith," an inheritance tax is imposed on the person receiving such benefit as if that person had received money equal to the value of the benefit received. Second, if a gift is made to a nonprofit organization and, in the determination of the Finance Ministry, the tax free transfer of that gift would result in "an improper reduction of the inheritance tax or gift burden of the relatives of the donator, legator, or other person who is in a special relationship with such donator or legator," the foundation will be treated as an individual and consequently must pay tax on the value of the "inherited" property. Inheritance Tax Law, Articles 65 and 66, Clauses 1 and 4.

17. The precise language of category 4 is: "contributions to public juristic persons, public interest juristic persons and other corporations incorporated by specific laws, including contributions to political or religious societies ('general contributions')."

18. At least with respect to sales of stock, block sales of less than a certain amount are tax free in Japan. Because many corporate foundation endowments consist of stock of the founding company, it seems that in actuality, tax may not have to be paid in conjunction with the contribution of appreciated stock to a foundation.

19. Thus a corporation that makes a contribution to other than the government, or a designated contribution, may be subject to tax on 100 percent of the gain but may not receive a corresponding deduction for the full amount if that amount would exceed the overall percentage limitations.

20. A similar prohibition exists in the United States, with the exception of some foreign charities granted an exception by tax treaty. One way around the restriction, in both Japan and the United States, is to contribute to domestic organizations that make grants or conduct programs internationally. The difference between this type of donation and the donations made through the Japan Foundation is that in the latter case, the donor can specifically select the recipient organization and can have its name attached to the gift.

21. See *The Japan Foundation: Outline/Annual Report for Fiscal 1987* (Tokyo: Japan Foundation, 1988), pp. 51–53.

22. Upon approval by the Ministry of Foreign Affairs, the specified funds are transferred to the Ministry of Finance which then officially increases the foundation's budget for the year (the Ministry of Finance, in general, must approve the annual budget appropriations for other ministries and, by extension, for the Japan Foundation) by the donated amount, thus enabling the foundation to transfer the funds overseas. As a result of this mechanical procedure, the timing of funding through the Japan Foundation must be coordinated with annual budget decisions by the Ministry of Finance.

23. Statistics provided to me by the Planning and Accounting Departments of the Japan Foundation.

This compares with only ¥531 million (approximately $3.8 million) in general (unspecified) contributions to the Japan Foundation during the same period.

24. See note 9 on the automatic granting of SPIPC status to certain types of nonprofit organization.

25. By contrast, the IRS, which is solely responsible for granting federal income tax exemption, maintains an internal list of such exempt organizations, and it annually publishes (and more frequently updates) a list of the hundreds of thousands of organizations eligible to receive tax-deductible contributions.

26. Of course, indirect ways of getting information do exist. For example, when a corporation makes contributions, it must list on its tax return the name and address of the organization(s) to which it has contributed. The Ministry of Finance can certainly cross-check the identified organizations, but because there is no system of taxpayer identification numbers in Japan, all such cross-checking must be done by manual (rather than computer) audit. This is a time-consuming and haphazard audit system at best.

27. Interview with Mr. Toshio Tojima, manager, Corporate Tax Division, National Tax Administration, November 10, 1986.

28. Ibid. Note that this survey was based on a sampling of approximately 6.3 percent of the total number of nonprofit organizations engaged in

business activities and filing tax returns with the NTA. Accordingly, this sampling represents only 0.4 percent of the total number of nonprofit organizations existing in Japan at the time of the survey.

29. Interview with Mr. Toshio Tojima, November 10, 1986.

30. Although guidance issued by the various ministries prohibits such practices, policing the expenses of nonprofit organizations is extremely difficult, given the decentralization of the system and the lack of computerized tax auditing.

31. It has never been demonstrated empirically that many of the violations targeted by the 1969 legislation were ever widespread in the United States, just as it has not been demonstrated to date that such abuses are prevalent in Japan. See Simon, "The Tax Treatment of Nonprofit Organizations," pp. 91–94. Nonetheless, the potential for such abuse was perceived to exist, and the adoption of the 1969 rules—however controversial many of them remain—has contributed to a more elevated view of private philanthropy in the United States than existed in the early 1960s. Because there is such a problem of perception with respect to the activities of Japanese nonprofit organizations, it may be that the best argument favoring the adoption of similar regulations (whether through the mechanism of the tax law or otherwise) would be to remove the tarnish from the current image of these organizations.

32. Significantly, these new regulations were to apply to private foundations only, for it was here, and here alone, that the public perceived the wealthy (whether corporate or individual) to be benefiting unjustly from the tax benefits provided in the Internal Revenue Code. Other nonprofit organizations, especially public charities, were not affected.

33. It is not always clear whether this reflects purely an informational problem or the larger, practical problem that even though many categories of non-science-oriented SPIPCs exist on the books, it may actually be difficult to obtain approval in nonscience areas without the "proper connections."

34. This type of hierarchy is quite familiar in U.S. system as well, in which nonprofit organizations fall into a hierarchy of four types of organizations: (1) noncharitable, nonprofit organizations, (2) public charities, (3) private operating foundations, and (4) private nonoperating (i.e., grant-making) foundations. As in Japan, the hierarchy affects the deductibility of contributions to these organizations and other regulatory matters. For example, organizations in Category 1 are exempt from tax but are not eligible to receive any deductible contributions; all organizations in Categories 2 through 4 can receive deductible contributions, but to differing extents—contributions to organizations in Categories 2 and 3 are generally deductible by individuals up to a limit of 50 percent of adjusted gross

income, and contributions to organizations in Category 3 are deductible only up to 30 percent; and organizations in Categories 1 and 2 are not subject to the preceding private foundation regulations, whereas those in Categories 3 and 4 are.

35. It also reflects a sense, expressed to me many times, that scientific organizations — through their research activities — contribute tangibly to the national welfare and thus merit tax subsidies, whereas the benefits of cultural organizations are more attenuated and thus harder to identify.

36. Interview with Mr. Toshio Tojima, November 10, 1986.

37. Ibid.

38. Ibid.

39. "Political Donations total ¥167.59 billion in 1986," *Japan Times* September 4, 1987, p. 2. The Home Affairs Ministry statistics are based on reports submitted to the ministry by 3,374 out of a total of 4,601 political bodies and organizations that are legally required to make such reports. Each political party or organization must report to the ministry all donations exceeding ¥10,000, and individual politicians must report each donation of over ¥1 million.

40. These recommendations were submitted in the fall of 1986, but as yet no concrete action has resulted. In fact, even at the time that the report was submitted, members of the study group were not optimistic about the likelihood of a positive response.

41. See, for example, J. Mark Davidson Schuster, "Supporting the Arts: An International Comparative Study" (study funded by the Policy and Planning Division, National Endowment for the Arts, March 1985); and Questionnaire of the Tax Incentives of Recipients and Donors for Contributions to Charitable Organizations in Various Countries (questionnaire prepared by Coopers & Lybrand and McLean & Co., June 1988).

42. Interview with Mr. Mikio Kato, March 16, 1987.

43. Interview with Mr. Natsuaki Fusano, general manager, Keidanren, November 27, 1986. See the discussion of Keidanren's role in charitable fund-raising in Chapter 6.

44. "The Charitable Behavior of Americans," The Independent Sector, p. 2.

45. For better or worse, the IRS is highly computerized. In addition to using taxpayer ID numbers to cross-check and verify information provided by taxpayers, the IRS has developed a computer system known as the Taxpayer Compliance Measurement Program for selecting tax returns for audit. Based on surveys of randomly selected and exhaustively examined tax returns, the IRS has developed confidential formulas that describe a "normal" tax return at specified income levels. These formulas are used in scanning incoming tax returns in order to determine whether a given return

deviates in any significant way from the defined norm. Those that do are automatically selected for review.

46. In September 1989, the Home Affairs Ministry announced plans to study the idea of assigning taxpayer ID numbers to individual and corporate taxpayers to help prevent tax evasion. The ministry hopes to submit a draft outline of the proposed system sometime in 1991, but the proposal is expected to generate a great deal of public opposition as an infringement on the privacy of individuals.

6

The Philanthropic Process—
Management, Operation,
and Grant Making

As the preceding two chapters have demonstrated, the legal and tax frameworks that shape Japanese philanthropy are the product of the unique Japanese cultural setting and hence are very different from those that give United States philanthropy its form. The internal procedures according to which grant-making foundations and corporate contributions programs govern themselves are also culturally derived, yet it is in this area that Japanese and U.S. foundations are most similar. Differences here seem to be predominantly those of degree rather than substance.

The similarities between Japanese and U.S. philanthropy in this regard are, unfortunately, not a compliment to either group, as a common observation about both Japanese and U.S. foundations is that in general they are rather conservative, lacking in creativity and innovation. Mr. Korenobu Takahashi, director of corporate and scientific programs for IBM Japan, observed that one of the prominent characteristics of Japanese corporate philanthropy is that it is "passive"—more passive, he felt, than its U.S. counterpart. By this he meant two things: First, Japanese corporate grant making is not very inventive or catalytic. Rather than making pioneering grants, foundations tend to allocate their largesse according to established paths, giving to safe, well-known, and established programs and often merely following the previous year's budget. Second, grants are overwhelmingly reactive, made in response to unsolicited requests, particularly from powerful business organizations, rather than in pursuit of a previously defined, clear giving strategy.

With respect to both concerns, the same could be and has been said about U.S. corporate grant making; that is, it is not always creative and is often reactive. Unfortunately, when Japanese foundations and grant makers compare themselves with their U.S. counterparts, they usually compare themselves with the biggest and best, even though the largest Japanese foundations are not nearly so large.[1] In particular, they tend to compare themselves with the foundations best known in Japan—Ford, Rockefeller, and Carnegie— which are not only among the better examples of U.S. philanthropy but which are also independent foundations for which there is no exact counterpart in Japan. If instead they compared themselves with the majority of smaller foundations and, in particular, with corporate foundations and corporate-giving programs rather than with independent foundations, their self-stigmatization as "passive" in comparison with American grant makers would begin to fade.

Waldemar Nielson has criticized even some of the largest U.S. foundations for being more reactive than active, noting: "Because most donors have envisioned their foundations as vehicles for the simple distribution of charitable gifts . . . they seldom attempt to take the lead in identifying and filling institutional gaps in society or in launching new experimental programs. The majority of them can be compared to bankers, waiting for loan applications to be presented; and like any careful banker, they tend to give preference to the applicants who are familiar, who can present good credentials, and who are generally 'sound'."[2] This portrait is equally apt for Japanese corporate foundations and direct donation programs.

In one respect, however, the "reactive" passivity of Japanese grant makers described by Mr. Takahashi does differ markedly from that of U.S. corporate donors, specifically in their responsiveness to grant solicitations from the Keidanren, Japan's largest and most powerful business association. Far from reacting generally to grant proposals from a host of nonprofit organizations, Japanese corporate donors rely heavily, and in many cases exclusively, on the Keidanren to evaluate and select appropriate fund recipients. This chapter will first examine the role of the Keidanren and other industrial associations in the corporate philanthropic process and then describe in general terms the operation of direct corporate-giving programs and corporate foundations.

The Keidanren and Corporate Giving

The most powerful and prestigious business organization in Japan, the Keidanren (Federation of economic organizations) is also the single most powerful organization in the fund-raising/grant-making field. In fiscal 1988 the Keidanren handled over sixty separate fund-raising requests for charitable causes, totaling ¥7.6 billion ($54 million).[3] It plays a role, both in business policymaking and in corporate philanthropy, for which there is no equivalent in the United States, and it heavily influences the course of corporate grant making in Japan.

The Keidanren is itself a nonprofit organization founded in 1946 to mobilize a consensus of business opinion and to represent that consensus in informing and influencing government policy. Today the Keidanren's membership consists of over 120 industrial, commercial, and financial associations and close to 900 corporations. In addition to its role as chief liaison between big business and government on policy matters, the Keidanren is a major source of political funding for the Liberal Democratic party, Japan's biggest and longest-governing party. Its role as a fund-raiser for charitable causes seems to be an outgrowth of its political fund-raising activities.

Mr. Natsuaki Fusano, one of the managing directors of the Keidanren, described the evolution of the Keidanren's philanthropic fund-raising:

> Modern-style grant making is really a phenomenon of the postwar era, and in particular, the post-1960s era. Before the war, to the extent this kind of activity existed at all, it was carried out by the zaibatsu and mostly for community events such as *matsuri* [festivals].[4] After the war, the zaibatsu were dissolved, and individual companies didn't feel strong enough to carry on on their own, so large industrial associations — steel, electric, railroad, banking — were formed. These became the successors to the zaibatsu in the fund-raising field, too. Because the Keidanren is the association of these associations, we have now undertaken the primary responsibility for fund-raising.[5]

In general, Keidanren does not raise funds or make grants on its own behalf. Instead, it acts as a middleman, brokering between grant seekers and potential donors. This is consistent with its political fund-raising role in which it also acts as intermediary, assessing its constituents a fixed amount for ultimate transmission to the Liberal Democratic party.

According to Mr. Fusano, the Keidanren offers three different levels of assistance to those seeking corporate funding, depending on the importance it attaches to the project. In most cases, Keidanren assistance is limited to giving fund-raisers a list of Keidanren corporate and association members who may be approached for a contribution—the "Keidanren list." Occasionally, Keidanren will go one step further and in addition to the Keidanren list will write a letter of introduction to the various corporations or associations on the list. Finally, in rare circumstances, the Keidanren will itself actively campaign for funds among its members on behalf of a third party.

Any organization, domestic or foreign, can seek Keidanren assistance—and many have done so—but not all will be successful. Mr. Fusano had a difficult time articulating the basis on which the Keidanren decides whom to help and to what degree. In fact, he indicated that the Keidanren employs no fixed set of objective standards at all but, rather, uses a *kimochi* approach, taking into account such factors as the general economic and political climate (particularly in regard to assisting overseas organizations); the size, scope, and prestige of the project; areas of particular need or concern; and an "informal feeling for government priorities."[6]

One example of this flexible approach is the Keidanren's relationship with the U.S.-based Japan Society. As I mentioned, it is extremely rare for the Keidanren to raise funds actively on behalf of any organization, particularly a non-Japanese organization, but the Keidanren does so on an ongoing basis for the Japan Society. According to Mr. Fusano, this degree of involvement is unique and is based mainly on a personal relationship and personal sense of obligation. "Of course," Mr. Fusano observed, "the Japan Society meets any possible objective concerns we could have (such as high prestige, issues of cross-cultural concern, political visibility and palatability), but the real basis for our assistance to the Japan Society is the personal relationship between the president of Keidanren and the Rockefeller family, the founders of the Japan Society, and also our gratitude for the vast amounts of Rockefeller money in various forms that were used to help Japan in the postwar period."[7]

Although most supplicants cannot expect the kind of advocacy practiced by the Keidanren on behalf of the Japan Society, their causes can be greatly advanced by Keidanren support on any level. Mere possession of the Keidanren list is no guarantee of success, but it is a valuable fund-raising tool, and combined with a letter of introduction, it can become quite an effective one.

The list itself is important because it contains the names of Keidanren member corporations and associations and also a suggested contribution percentage (a percentage of the total sum sought, not a fixed dollar or yen amount) for each member, based on what Mr. Fusano and others referred to as the "Keidanren formula." Thus, an organization in possession of the list knows both whom to approach and approximately how much it may reasonably request. Although companies do not always give the amounts desired, they do seem to comply in general with Keidanren solicitations. Fund-raisers have indicated that they may only get half the amount they request from any company, but usually the gifts will be in proportion to the percentages appearing on the Keidanren list.

Neither Mr. Fusano nor anyone else could explain exactly how these target percentages are determined, except to explain that they are based loosely on a formula taking into account the members' average annual income over a period of approximately five years and their capital. Of the two factors, Mr. Fusano indicated that capital is the more important, as Keidanren's experience over the years has indicated that corporate giving does not tend to vary significantly with fluctuations in income but, rather, seems to be linked to capital.[8]

Keidanren members that are themselves industrial or business associations also use a formula approach to assess each of their members a proportionate share of the amount that they are assessed by Keidanren, but the actual formula varies from association to association. Thus, for example, the auto industry association bases its calculation on the number of cars sold or produced by each of its member companies; the steel association bases its calculation on volume of pig iron production; the electric power association bases its formula on the volume of electricity produced; and the bank association bases its formula on the magnitude of either loans or deposits.

Aside from being a help to the potential donee, possession of the Keidanren list (or being approached by a fund-raiser in possession of the list) is also a help to the potential donors. Because of the group orientation prevalent in Japan, companies prefer to know how comparable companies—competitors and compatriots—have reacted or will react to a grant proposal before they commit themselves, lest they become conspicuous for either overcontributing or undercontributing. The Keidanren list gives them this information. Although the Keidanren percentages are merely a guideline, companies seem to adhere to them precisely because they offer a measure of predictability.

According to Mr. Kumagai of the Hitachi Corporation: "In this regard, Japan is still a place of small local villages, as it was years ago. Companies give in response to an industry or association request, in order to be part of their village or community, as they used to give when the zaibatsu asked. They don't want to stand out for good or for bad."[9]

"Community" plays a role in the grant decisions of U.S. corporations as well, although in a less structured, formalized way. It has been observed that in the United States, whatever a firm's level of managerial commitment to charitable giving is, if its business community considers generous giving an obligation, the firm will tend to be more responsive. In addition, firms influence one another's giving policies. They are generally well informed about the policies of other companies and tend to increase their own giving when other firms in the same region increase their contributions. In a 1981 survey of major U.S. companies, two-thirds of the companies reported that peer comparisons were a very important influence on their own giving decisions, ranking equally with the substantive nature of the appeal.[10] Unlike the Keidanren approach, however, U.S. corporations tend to learn about and influence one another's practices informally, through meetings and contacts between contributions and public affairs managers, rather than through the maintenance of lists and giving formulas.

In addition to providing the means for interchange (and the basis for security) within the corporate community, the Keidanren role in fund-raising relieves corporations from the need to make grant-making decisions themselves and eliminates the risk of making a bad or embarrassing choice, something that again would mean a loss of face in the community. As we shall see, most corporations have not allocated enough staff or financial resources for full-fledged giving programs, and consequently their ability to evaluate carefully a variety of proposals is severely limited. A Keidanren endorsement of a particular project, as evidenced by a letter of introduction or a direct appeal, to a great extent absolves companies of responsibility with respect to individual grant requests.

The closest parallel in the U.S. context to this facet of the Keidanren role would be "federated giving" through organizations like the United Way. Corporations regard this type of giving as "safe," involving little risk of controversy or failure. Despite the comfort that federated giving offers, however, corporate giving to the United Way and other similar organizations has been on the decline in recent years.[11] One reason may be that corporations feel they receive too little recognition, either within the business community or among shareholders and customers, for this type of generalized giving. A similar concern on the part of Japanese corporations may already be having an impact on the Keidanren's pivotal fund-raising role.

As with many things in Japan, the Keidanren system of fund-raising and corporate reliance on it is changing in response to the pressures of a changed world and, in particular, in response to increasing worldwide demand for Japanese philanthropic funds. Interestingly, the question of whether the expansion of Japanese philanthropy has led to a larger or smaller role for the Keidanren elicits diametrically opposed responses. Mr. Fusano feels that reliance on Keidanren has increased, whereas Mr. Tadashi Yamamoto (Japan Center for International Exchange) and others speculate that Keidanren's influence in this area may be waning. The real answer appears to be that both answers are correct, depending on which sector of the corporate economy one is using as a point of reference.

Mr. Fusano's view is that corporations are being overwhelmed by unprecedented numbers of requests for funds, especially from overseas organizations. In particular, Keidanren's traditional members—the big steel, manufacturing, and railroad companies— are unprepared to deal with grant proposals from foreign sources, for which the difficulties are compounded by linguistic and cultural nuances. As a result they have turned increasingly to the Keidanren for help. In addition, these companies, which are largely in the manufacturing and wholesale sector, are not as eager for the public-relations benefit of grant making as the more consumer-oriented companies might be.

According to Mr. Yamamoto, traditional Keidanren member companies are motivated more by an old-fashioned sense of community and sense of obligation to return to society some of the benefits they have enjoyed (*on* and *giri*). "These are the companies that have grown rich with the active support of the government, especially under various subsidy and incentive programs implemented after the war. Therefore they have a close relationship with the government and a feeling of obligation to the government for its past and continuing patronage. They are happy to accept anonymity as granters in exchange for being insulated from the outstretched hands of the grantees."[12]

On the other hand, heavy industries are declining, and some observers feel that consequently, Keidanren's power is also waning or at least is being redefined. At the same time, newer and more maverick high-tech, electronics, and financial services companies are on the rise. These companies have never been the locus of Keidanren power and hence have a looser affiliation with that organization. Moreover, according to Mr. Yamamoto, unlike heavy industries, these companies do not feel that they were specially nurtured by the government and so do not feel the same measure of societal obligation or at least do not feel that they need to express it quietly. They are more aggressively consumer and market oriented, and their grant-making strategies reflect that fact. They want the public-relations bang for their buck.

As the relevant definition of community for these more maverick Japanese companies expands across national and international borders, they are worrying less about loss of face than their industrial forebears did and are striking out more often and more aggressively on their own. Nonetheless, though the influence of Keidanren may not pervade in this sector, it certainly still exists. Recent developments, in fact, point to a new role for the Keidanren in the overseas business community that may ultimately parallel its crucial domestic role.

In 1988, the Keidanren formed an affiliate organization in the United States called the Council for Better Investment in the United

States, under the leadership of Mr. Akio Morita, chairman of the Sony Corporation. As the name of the organization suggests, the idea behind its founding is to foster a better political environment for Japanese investment in the United States by exploring means for eliminating trade and investment friction. One of these means is to promote "good corporate citizenship." The council has already sponsored seminars on improving community relations and, in particular, has focused on educating Japanese companies about affirmative action and grant-making options that support minority groups.[13] In keeping with the Keidanren's fund-raising role, the council has begun coordinating contributions by Japanese companies, with the United Negro College Fund and the National Hispanic Scholarship Fund being among the first beneficiaries. It would seem, then, that even in the new, more aggressive, international business community, some of the important, traditional concepts and patterns of corporate philanthropy are being adapted and maintained.

Corporate-giving Programs

Precisely because they do not have a separate legal or psychological identity, direct corporate-giving programs in Japan are the most likely to be "passive" in both of the respects suggested by IBM Japan's Mr. Takashi: They are not very innovative, and they respond to the fund-raising requests of the Keidanren and its constituent industrial and business associations rather than independently seeking grant-making opportunities.

As in the United States, most corporate giving is handled through the general or public affairs department, or *sōmubu*, which serves an amalgam of public relations, political liaison, personnel, and interdepartmental coordination functions. According to Mr. Masaaki Wakao, a former general affairs manager and director at the Sony Corporation, the *sōmubu*'s role encompasses everything from buying flowers for an employee's birthday to maintaining smooth relationships within the company and between the company and the government.[14] The importance of the latter function correlates directly to the size and importance of the company and includes responsibility for corporate political contributions. When a corpo-

108 JAPANESE CORPORATE PHILANTHROPY

ration has a foundation in addition to direct giving activities, the *sōmubu*'s office usually has oversight and coordination responsibilities for the foundation as well. Mr. Yamamoto pointed out that one of the *sōmubu*'s major functions is to coordinate the various departments of large companies, a role essential to building consensus with respect to corporate contributions as well as other corporate activities.

It is probably safe to say that no corporation in Japan has a professional staff devoted solely to philanthropic functions. Because the *sōmubu*'s office has so much else of a diverse nature to keep it occupied, it is not surprising that even with the best of intentions, grant-making decisions are often passive, reactive, and *ad hoc*. The corporate representatives with whom I talked followed no consistent, formal pattern in making grant determinations, probably because they had no formal, planned program of giving. Significantly, none of the corporations that I interviewed had a written statement of purpose or goal for their direct giving efforts, nor were corporations able to articulate orally their contributions goals, yet studies in the United States indicate that a well-defined company contributions policy is one of the key ingredients in successful, creative corporate-giving programs.[15]

All in all, it would be difficult to say that many Japanese corporations have giving "programs." What they do have, in general, is a willingness and ability to make contributions *ad hoc* in response to requests from appropriate sources.[16] How then are requests evaluated and determinations made? The three major factors on which most evaluations seem to be based, probably in increasing order of importance, are the merits of the project on its face, the benefit (in terms of publicity, access to facilities or information) to the company, and who makes the request. These factors are interrelated, and their relative importance depends on the particular case and the type of company to which the request is presented.

To say that the merits of a project are the least important factor is perhaps misleading. It is not that the merits are unimportant but, rather, that most companies — because they lack professional staff — lack the time and ability to assess them in depth. It is in this regard that the Keidanren plays one of its most important philanthropic roles. By acting as middleman between recipient organizations and corporate donors, it effectively prescreens and prejudges grant proposals, allowing only those deemed worthy to filter down to the individual corporations. Although companies indicated that they do not automatically and uncritically follow the Keidanren's suggestions, a strong Keidanren commitment (as evidenced by the Keidanren's active fund-raising or letters of introduction) in itself suggests to the company that the project has merit.[17] It also suggests that other companies will similarly be asked to contribute, and so the "group" dynamics described in previous chapters is called in to play.

As we have indicated, the emphasis on the public-relations benefit in return for a contribution varies with the type of company involved. Thus consumer-oriented companies look for recognition, however attenuated, from the consuming public and direct their giving accordingly. The Suntory Company (a major Japanese beverage producer and distributor) is one such company and was often cited by others as being outside the norm for Japanese-style philanthropy. The strong implication was that Suntory is perhaps too market oriented. Within Suntory and other similar companies, however, this type of aggressive grant making is viewed very favorably as active rather than passive and innovative rather than repetitious. By contrast, traditional Keidanren member companies and associations seem to be more concerned about recognition within the business community for doing their share and less preoccupied with consumer-oriented public-image issues.

In addition to the boon to public and community relations, many companies seek a more concrete and direct benefit in return for their donations. Numerous American fund-raisers expressed surprise at the straightforward—some would say blatant—quid pro quo demands made in connection with the Japanese companies' consideration of grant proposals. One fund-raiser for a major U.S. university reported that he was confounded that although "they [Japanese company representatives] never once raised the issue of whether their contribution would be tax deductible, they were very up front about what they expected in return for a contribution: They wanted access to one of our major high-tech labs—all of this in exchange for a contribution that was not very significant in dollar terms."[18]

Mr. Eichi Furukawa, a former Japanese government official, explained this attitude: "Japanese companies do not yet understand the concept of pure voluntarism. Everything is premised on *on* and *giri*. When a request is made and fulfilled, a return obligation is created and must be repaid. That is the way corporate philanthropy works today in Japan."[19]

The centrality of traditional *on/giri* relationships to corporate grant-making decisions is apparent not only in the expectation that a benefit commensurate with the gift should be forthcoming but also in the importance attached by corporations to the source of the grant request, for *on* and *giri* run both ways. That is, grants are often made by corporations in response to, and largely on the basis of, a request by an individual with whom the corporation has a relationship and toward whom the corporation feels some debt of gratitude. Keidanren's fund-raising for the Japan Society fits squarely in this mold.

There is also a more practical explanation for the importance attached to the source of a grant request. Because they lack staff trained in making grants, companies often substitute their personal regard for and faith in an individual for a detailed scrutiny of a project's merits. Thus, Mr. Yamamoto related the story of his efforts to set up and fund an exchange of experts concerned with energy issues:

> I first approached a well-known Diet member who is involved in energy issues. With his support and a letter of introduction from the Keidanren, I then went to the Association of Electric Power Companies to present my proposal. Although the head of the association was in favor of the concept, he said it would have to be presented "correctly" to the association members if I wanted to raise any money. His idea of the "correct" presentation was to have the Diet member himself make the pitch. We went back and forth several times, and finally the Diet member did make a presentation to the association, and we got our funding. In this case, the association really didn't care about the merits of the project.[20]

The view of corporate contributions as part of the crisscrossing maze of *on/giri* relationships also has an impact on the types of projects that corporations are willing to support. Most corporate grants are allocated to projects of no more than a year's duration, although in some cases they may be renewable for up to three years. This seems consistent with the notion that the grant is a repayment—

a lump sum, if you will—for some benefit received, rather than a long-term investment in a policy, cause, or organization.

Our discussion has centered on the criteria that influence the rather improvised donations decisions of Japanese corporations. The actual mechanics of decision making, however, are extremely difficult to define. This is true of the entire corporate decision-making process, not just that small portion relating to philanthropy. To the extent that patterns can be discerned, they tend to be similar to those followed by corporate foundations, as described in the following section.

Corporate Foundations

Almost all foundations in Japan are corporate foundations. Although the degree of their independence from their parent companies varies tremendously, they do have separate corporate structures and identities. Even though their giving patterns have also been described as passive, foundations are not as reactive as are the corporations themselves. Foundations are required by law to have at least a general written statement of purpose (in the articles of endowment) and to demonstrate to the government's satisfaction that they have allocated sufficient financial resources to carry out those purposes. At the very least, this makes their giving more focused, coherent, and purposeful, although not necessarily more creative, than direct corporate giving.

Like their U.S. counterparts, Japanese corporate foundations are nonshareholder corporations run by officers and governed by a board of directors (*rijikai*). Although only a board of directors is required by the Civil Code, most Japanese foundations are also governed by a board of counselors (*hyōginkai*). As the name implies, the role of the latter is intended to be advisory rather than functional, although the board of counselors often has nominal authority for approving the annual budget and program plans. The principal significance of both the board of directors and the board of counselors (and particularly the counselors) is to give the foundation status and visibility in the community, and accordingly the members are selected from among business, academic, and often government leaders.

The composition of both boards and the rules governing the frequency and content of their meetings are largely determined by the government ministry under which the foundation is established. The Civil Code itself contains only skeletal requirements, and even these are often modified by the ministry. In order to preserve the independence (or at least the appearance of independence) of the foundation from the corporate parent, most ministries restrict the number of foundation board members who may at the same time be company board members.[21] In general, the members of the board of counselors elect members of the board of trustees and vice versa, usually for a term of two years.

Independence from the supervising ministry is another matter. Many ministries require or "request" that the board of directors (and/or the board of counselors) contain at least one member or former member of that ministry, a system that has both advantages and disadvantages, as it enables the ministry to keep an eye on the foundation and even to assist it but may expose the foundation to undue government influence.

In general, both the board of directors and the board of counselors meet twice a year, once to approve grants and plan the next year's programs and once at the end of the fiscal year to prepare the following year's budget. For the most part, boards merely approve the recommendations forwarded to them by the foundation staff and/or by specially appointed selection committees. As Mr. Mikio Kato commented: "Board members don't feel that they have or are supposed to have any active and continuing role once the foundation has been set up. Their names and reputations are necessary for establishing the foundation and for lending it continuing respectability, but they themselves have no real substantive responsibility. They are supporting actors, not stars."[22] Similar observations have been made about the trustees of U.S. foundations. Waldemar Nielson observed: "In legal theory, the legitimacy of the institution of private philanthropy rests on the principle of trusteeship. But if in reality the performance of philanthropy depended on the effectiveness of the boards of trustees, it would truly be in trouble. Their mechanism of governance is considered . . . to be the weakest element in the structure."[23]

Of course, in the best examples of philanthropy, board members take their roles seriously and contribute conscientiously to the development of foundation policy and activities. In the United States, the development of this type of positive, active role has largely been linked to the evolution of the foundations themselves. When the foundation donor is alive and active, the trustees tend to be no more than a rubber stamp. In a different scenario, if the predominant board group consists of the executives of a donor company, the trustees may behave predominantly as guardians of the company's reputation, deflecting any controversial foundation behavior that could tarnish the company's public image. Once the donor has died, the donor's family has lost interest in the foundation, and/or the company has been separated from the foundation, the trustees are free to adopt a more independent, less conflicted stance.[24]

Because most Japanese foundations are corporate foundations and, more importantly, because most that are active today were formed since 1965, they have not yet reached the stage in their evolution of meaningful separation from their donors. It may be this factor, more than any other, that limits the role and effectiveness of their governing boards.

As with many other government guidelines, ministry requirements relating to the governing boards of nonprofit organizations are negotiable, within limits. Mr. Seiichi Mitani, executive director of the Mitsubishi Bank Foundation, feeling that a board of counselors was an unnecessary and duplicative formality, successfully persuaded the Ministry of Foreign Affairs to forgo that particular requirement at the time of the foundation's incorporation. Similarly, Mr. Chosei Kabira, of the Hōsō-bunka Foundation (Broadcast [NHK] cultural foundation), reported that he repeatedly rejected bids by the Ministry of Posts and Telecommunications to place a current ministry representative on his board.[25]

Although the process of negotiating standards for management structure is time-consuming, having once established them, foundations did not find either the standards or the boards themselves particularly vexing or problematic. By contrast, virtually all of the foundations that I surveyed felt concerned, frustrated, and hampered by a single, shared problem—staff or, rather, the lack of sufficient and sufficiently competent staff. This was uniformly cited as the major obstacle hindering foundation growth and limiting the caliber of foundation work in Japan.

Mr. Tom Fox of the Council on Foundations pointed out that this may be another instance of the Japanese comparing themselves unfairly and unfavorably to the biggest and best U.S. foundations, for overall only 7 percent of the approximately 26,000 foundations in the United States have at least one part-time or full-time paid employee.[26] These statistics change dramatically depending on the size of the foundation. U.S. corporate foundations that have assets exceeding $1 million or that give at least $100,000 in contributions averaged 3.5 paid staff in 1987, whereas independent foundations meeting the same criteria averaged 4.9 paid staff.[27] All of the Japanese foundations that I interviewed would have met these financial criteria, yet almost without exception, their staffs consisted of no more than one or two individuals.[28] Even though these represent some of the largest foundations in Japan, set up by companies with ample financial resources, they still felt that they lacked staff—and more importantly the autonomy to appoint appropriate staff—to carry out existing programs, much less to branch out and be more creative.

More determinative than mere numbers, however, is the fact that far from being trained professionals, most foundation employees in Japan are lent by the parent company on either a part-time or full-time basis, with no apparent connection between the work they were doing in the company and the skills required by the foundation. These temporary appointments, or *shukkō* last for about two to four years, at which point the employees return to the company. Unfortunately, as Mr. Masayuki Deguchi of the Suntory Foundation noted, this rotation system means that just at the point that the staff have gained some experience, they are returned to the company, and their expertise is lost to the foundation.[29]

What is more troubling, according to Ms. Yoshiko Wakayama of the Toyota Foundation, is that the people selected to staff foundations are not generally regarded by the company as top people. "They are not on [the fast] track. Look around and you will see that the typical foundation staff are either about to reach retirement age or in some way just don't fit the company image. Moreover, they have no training in philanthropy and even less interest in it, as they know that they will shortly be returning to the company."[30] In one case, a foundation president told me that his sole staff person is a middle-aged, handicapped man for whom the company could find no suitable position internally, and so he was given to the foundation.

Naturally, the employees themselves are aware of staffing hierarchies and thus often regard it as no great honor to be selected for foundation duty. This, according to Mr. Yujiro Hayashi, is a major failing of the nonprofit system, because "one sign of social maturity is the degree to which the third sector is firmly established. By 'firmly established' I am not referring simply to percentages of working population or percentages of income; I am focusing on a more important issue: the extent to which people engaged in third-sector occupations feel pride in their work and consider their jobs a reason for living. Viewed from this standpoint, Japan can scarcely be said to have attained social maturity."[31]

The foundations themselves have very little involvement with staff selection, which is handled almost entirely and unilaterally by the corporate personnel department. In one case, a foundation manager told me that he had approached the personnel department about hiring someone from outside the company, as "the company was unwilling to give me even one person of any caliber from within. They told me that if I wanted to hire someone, it would be entirely my responsibility, and that if things didn't work out for the employee or for me, I could expect no help from the personnel department."[32] This problem is compounded because the corporation often pays the salary of staff on loan to the foundation but will not necessarily do so if someone is hired from outside.

Largely because of the limitations of staff, most foundations rely on specially appointed selection committees to review grant proposals and recommend grant recipients. Selection committees are composed of scholars or other experts in the field of the foundation's grant-making activities. Members generally have no formal connection to the company and are usually appointed by the board of directors for a two-year period, renewable indefinitely. Although staff may do some initial screening of grant applications or a subsequent review of the recommendations of the selection committees, it is these committees that do most of the substantive work of awarding grants.

Once the selection committee has made its recommendations, those suggestions are usually reviewed, at least formally, by the staff, which in turn makes recommendations to the board. Unlike the United States, where studies have indicated that chief executive officers (CEOs) often get quite involved in contributions decisions and where CEO commitment is probably the most important element in the overall success of the corporation's contributions program, the CEO in Japan is not an obvious factor in the foundation's activity.[33] It seems, however, that the CEO looms large, albeit in the background. It is true in general in Japan that decisions are made more on a basis of consensus than at the direction of the CEO, but if one asks those responsible for building this consensus they will say that they do so with a pretty clear knowledge of the CEOs preferences. In this, it seems that corporate foundations are no exception. The staff and selection committees do not operate in a vacuum, but with a firm understanding of the executive management's priorities.

The use and composition of selection committees form an interesting point of comparison with the United States, where corporate foundations also rely on appointed committees for a good deal of their substantive work but where such committees generally consist of corporate, management-level employees. These committees vary greatly in their composition, stature, and mode of operation, but they generally provide critical support to contributions managers and staff. It could be said that the use of such internal committees, as opposed to the Japanese use of outside experts, merely serves to entrench the corporate self-interest, but it has been found that in most cases these committees have considerable authority and take their work seriously.[34] Moreover, participation on such committees increases the exposure of corporate employees to the corporation's activities in this area and enables them to influence company policy.[35]

It would seem that the involvement of staff, and particularly of management, on selection committees in Japanese foundations would substantially contribute to the much-needed growth in public awareness of private philanthropy, but there is a bit of a chicken-and-egg problem in that until philanthropy is widely accepted, employees do not want to participate. In 1986, Ms. Martha Montag-Brown, then manager of community affairs at Levi-Strauss, came to Japan hoping to establish a corporate contributions program that would parallel in some measure the programs that Levi-Strauss has established in the United States and elsewhere overseas. These programs are well known for their creative and active reliance on employees' initiatives. Ms. Montag-Brown surveyed the Levi-Strauss Japan employees to find out how they would like to structure a local program and found to her surprise and dismay that there was very little enthusiasm for the idea of employees participating at all. The major stumbling blocks seemed to be a hesitancy by individual employees to take responsibility for the expenditure of company funds (see Chapter 2), a fear that such undertakings would not truly be acceptable to management, and a concern about how allocating time to contributions activities would influence their career advancement. Therefore, until there is sufficient executive-level commitment to address these concerns, it seems likely that selection committees will continue to be composed of outside experts.

Although the selection committees relieve pressure on otherwise insufficient foundation staff and provide necessary substantive expertise, some people feel that they contribute to the passivity and complacency of the grant process. Because many selection committee members are affiliated with universities or research institutions, there is a tendency for the same group of institutions to be favored with foundation grants year after year. In fact, most foundations do not publicize the availability of grant funds on a broad scale. Instead, they tend to advertise by word of mouth (often the "mouth" of selection committee members) or by selective notification of certain schools and research facilities.

Inbreeding among granters and grantees is not unique to Japan (in the United States it is widely acknowledged that powerful corporate executives are often invited to sit on the boards of eleemosynary institutions precisely because of their connections to sources of funds — from their own corporate till and others), although perhaps the extent and tenor of it are. Involvement of any kind with total strangers is unsettling for most Japanese, as I pointed out in Chapter 2, and this feeling carries over into the grant-making realm. Foundations find it much more reassuring to contribute to an established organization that has some connection to someone, that is, a selection committee or board member who has some connection to the foundation. Thus, Japanese continually express amazement at the kind of blind mail solicitation fund-raising that is customary in the United States. This would be (and has in fact proved to be), to a great extent, anathema in Japan.

The reluctance to risk the unknown that is reflected in the use of rather predictable selection committees also influences the types of grants that are made, and according to Mr. Mikio Kato, helps explain why prizes are a popular form of grant in Japan:

Very little is at stake here. Some prominent person is given an award for excellence. The company gets a lot of publicity; it holds a prize ceremony and invites the press. Unfortunately, however, these kinds of grants just reward past performance. They don't stimulate growth or encourage new discoveries.

Risk taking should be a very important facet of foundation activities, but almost no foundations in Japan see it this way. In this regard, foundations resemble the government and its budgeting process. Their resources are thin so all they do is look at last year's programs and decide whether the programs should get more or less money this year. Instead of making real, often hard choices, they err on the side of trying to please everyone.[36]

Another advantage of prizes as a form of grant is that they do not require subsequent oversight, supervision, or evaluation. One of the weakest links in U.S. grant making is postgrant evaluation. In Japan, too, there is very little evaluation of the grants although the need for such evaluation is, to a certain degree, negated by the fact that grants are so often made to known organizations or individuals. Moreover, according to one grant maker, the desirability of such scrutiny in many cases is debatable: "Here, because grants are so often made on the basis of a relationship or preexisting obligation, they are often regarded as gifts or repayments. Certainly when you give a gift to someone it would be terribly gauche to ask them how they liked it, used it, or spent it."[37]

As we stated at the beginning of this chapter, it is in the philanthropic process (as opposed to legal or tax structure) that Japanese and U.S. foundations most resemble each other. However, we should emphasize that what has been compared in the preceding pages is predominantly U.S. and Japanese corporate philanthropy. Although much of what we have said about the conservatism of the corporate philanthropic process and corporate foundations could and has been said about independent foundations in the United States, it is still true that corporate philanthropy has more pragmatic goals and is more constrained by a variety of financial and accountability concerns than are independent endeavors—whether private or institutional. Thus, the difference between the United States and Japan in this regard relates primarily to the impact of corporate philanthropy rather than the nature of it, because in the United States, corporate philanthropy accounts for only a tiny percentage of total charitable giving, whereas in Japan it represents the lion's share.

Notes

1. The largest foundation in Japan today is the Japan Shipbuilding Industry Foundation, with assets of approximately $1.5 billion. This foundation is about five times the size of its next largest competitor, the Sasakawa Peace Foundation (which is intended to have an endowment of $350 million but has not yet reached its full funding) but is still only one-quarter of the size of the Ford Foundation, the largest private foundation in the United States. Although the Japan Shipbuilding Industry Foundation is often referred to as a private foundation, it has very close ties with the Ministry of Transportation, under whose auspices it is incorporated.

2. Waldemar Nielson, *The Big Foundations* (New York: Columbia University Press, 1972), p. 275.

3. The source of this information is the Keidanren. Of the ¥7.6 billion, about ¥5.2 billion was for domestic programs and ¥2.4 billion was for international programs.

4. *Zaibatsu* is the term used to describe the huge industrial conglomerates that dominated Japanese business before World War II. The zaibatsu were officially disbanded by General Douglas MacArthur during the U.S. Occupation of Japan.

5. Interview with Mr. Natsuaki Fusano, managing director, Keidanren, November 27, 1986.

6. *Kimochi* is an often-used and very-difficult-to-define Japanese term, vaguely meaning, "feeling" or "mood," not in the sense of something whimsical or arbitrary, but rather, something more heartfelt.

7. Interview with Mr. Natsuaki Fusano, November 27, 1986.

8. It is not surprising that the Keidanren formula would take corporate capital into account, for the limit on deductibility of corporate contributions is calculated with respect to both capital and income, as we pointed out in the preceding chapter. Thus, although it was never specifically stated, it would seem that the Keidanren formula for establishing appropriate corporate giving levels may try, in some measure, to approximate deductibility.

It is interesting that Mr. Fusano felt that corporate giving in Japan is not greatly dependent on income. In the United States, annual corporate giving varies tremendously based on corporate profitability. This too is probably linked to the tax deduction structure, which is based on a percentage of pretax income. The difference between Japan and the United States in this regard may also have to do with differing time horizons and differing levels of accountability to shareholders. U.S. corporations are more sensitive to short-term profitability and the need to report that profitability on a quarterly basis to their shareholders than are their Japanese counterparts who have no such requirement and therefore may be better equipped to maintain funding levels even in bad business years.

9. Interview with Mr. Kazuo Kumagai, general manager, secretary's office, Hitachi Corporation, November 21, 1986.

10. See Michael Useem, "Corporate Philanthropy," in Walter W. Powell, ed., *The Non-Profit Sector: A Research Handbook* (New Haven, Conn.: Yale University Press, 1987), p. 350.

11. Donations to the United Way and other federated campaigns decreased from 22 percent of corporate gifts to 13 percent between 1976 and 1984. See L. Platzer, *Survey of Corporate Contributions, 1988 Edition* (New York: Conference Board, 1988), p. 22.

12. Interview with Mr. Tadashi Yamamoto, president of the Japan Center for International Exchange, August 16, 1986.

13. The latter is in direct response to the charges of racism that have arisen as the result not only of employment discrimination suits brought against Japanese companies in the United States but also of the derogatory remarks made by former Prime Minister Nakasone in 1986 about the education level of U.S. minorities.

14. Interview with Mr. Masaaki Wakao, August 16, 1986.

15. See E. B. Knauft, *Profiles of Effective Corporate Giving Programs* (New Haven, Conn.: Yale University, Program on Non-Profit Organizations, 1985).

In 1970, only a handful of large U.S. companies maintained any kind of formal public affairs department, but by 1980 all that had changed. A survey of the corporate contributions process conducted in 1980–1981 revealed widespread formalization of the giving process and integration of giving policy into company planning at the highest level. Eighty percent of 240 major firms surveyed in 1980–1981 had adopted formal policies on gifts, and 60 percent had issued written policies. See Useem, "Corporate Philanthropy," p. 344, citing John J. Siegfried, Katherine Maddox McElroy, and Diane Biernot-Fawkes, "The Management of Corporate Contributions," in Lee Preston, ed., *Research in Corporate Social Performance and Policy*, vol. 5 (Greenwich, Conn.: JAI Press, 1983).

16. At present this pattern is repeating itself in the giving programs of Japanese companies in the United States. A survey conducted by Yoshihiro Kondoh, a business graduate student at the University of Southern California, of members of the Japan Business Association of Southern California revealed the following: (1) Only 23 percent of the companies surveyed had assigned a specific person to handle grant requests. Only three companies had public relations departments, but in those three cases the public rela-

tions department coordinated giving. (2) Eighty-four percent of the companies have no formal criteria for screening grant proposals but instead react on an *ad hoc* basis (65 percent) or base their decisions on a previous year's record (19 percent). Yoshihiro Kondoh, "Evaluation of Japanese Corporate Contributions in the United States," manuscript, June 1987.

In contrast, most of the Japanese corporate foundations in the United States have been established with significant endowments and display a high degree of professionalism. They operate under established guidelines and employ at least one full-time manager (usually the foundation director), who is responsible for charitable contributions.

17. This is the dual merit of the project itself and of obtaining recognition in the business community for having responded faithfully to the Keidanren's request.

18. Details of the interview withheld at the request of the interviewee. It is far from unknown for American contributors to have similar expectations, but fund-raisers seemed to feel that expectations in Japan were higher, more firmly stated, and more directly linked to the amount that they were willing to contribute.

19. Interview with Mr. Eichii Furukawa, September 16, 1987.

20. Interview with Mr. Tadashi Yamamoto, president, The Japan Center for International Exchange, January 27, 1987.

21. In this regard, Japanese foundations are more independent (at least formally) of their parent companies than U.S. corporate foundations are. There is no similar stipulation in the United States requiring the separation of corporate and foundation governing bodies. In fact, almost all corporate foundation boards have significantly overlapping membership with the corporation's own board.

In practice, though, this difference may not exist. In response to my inquiries, I learned that there are no restrictions imposed by any of the ministries on the number of board members who may be directors or CEOs of related companies or of major corporate shareholders. Given Japan's unusual system of formally and informally interlocking companies and directorates, this leaves a fair amount of latitude for appointing "friendly" directors.

22. Interview with Mr. Mikio Kato, March 16, 1987.

23. Waldemar Nielson, *The Golden Donors* (New York: Dutton, 1985), p. 413.

24. Ibid., p. 414.

25. Interview with Mr. Seiichi Mitani, executive director Mitsubishi Bank Foundation, September 26, 1986; Interview with Mr. Chosei Kabira, executive secretary, Hōsō-bunka Foundation, October 6, 1986.

26. *1988 Foundation Management Report* (Washington, D.C.: Council on Foundations, 1988), p. 70.

27. *The Foundation Directory, 11th ed.* (New York: Foundation Center, 1987), pp. xi–xii.

28. Of the twenty corporate foundations that I interviewed, only the Toyota Foundation and the Suntory Foundation had more staff. Although the Toyota Foundation is technically a "corporate" foundation, it views itself more as an independent foundation, and its functioning and organization support that view.

29. Interview with Mr. Masayuki Deguchi, Suntory Foundation, August 4, 1986.

Note, however, that even in Japanese corporations, it is common for personnel to be shifted and for responsibilities to be altered every few years. This is also true in the government bureaucracy, and so in this regard, foundation staffing is not unique. This practice is also common in U.S. corporate foundations and giving programs, in which opinion is divided on its effects. Some feel that temporary appointments create a distinct lack of professionalism and unnecessary loss of expertise, and others feel that exposing more company employees to the firm's charitable activities ultimately strengthens the support for and quality of such activities.

30. Interview with Ms. Yoshiko Wakayama, international program director, Toyota Foundation, July 29, 1986.

31. Yujiro Hayashi, "Before the Dawn," p. 8. Although the numbers, professionalism, and prestige of foundation employees have improved dramatically in the United States since the 1960s, viewed from Professor Hayashi's standpoint in 1972, the United States would also have been considered lacking in social maturity. At that time, Waldemar Nielson observed that "there is hardly another comparable field of activity that is subject to so much disparagement by its clientele . . . in the academic and scientific community foundations officers are often considered second-rate individuals. . . . Although many government officials view foundation employment at times with envy, they also think of it as a refuge for people who have retired to the periphery of affairs." *The Big Foundations*, p. 323.

32. Details of the interview withheld at the request of the interviewee.

33. See Useem, "Corporate Philanthropy," pp. 340–359; Knauft, *Profiles of Effective Corporate Giving Programs*; Benjamin Lord, *Corporate Philanthropy in America: New Perspectives for the Eighties* (Washington, D.C.: Taft Corporation, 1984).

34. Knauft, *Profiles of Effective Corporate Giving Programs*, pp. 6–8.

35. One study found that the incidence of some degree of connection between corporate employees and recipient organizations was 30 percent or more. See Lord, *Corporate Philanthropy in America*, p. 12.

36. Interview with Mr. Mikio Kato, March 16, 1987.

37. Details of the interview withheld at the request of the interviewee.

7

Recent Developments and Future Directions

In the preceding chapters I have attempted to illustrate and support the contention that even when extending beyond the borders of Japan, Japanese philanthropy functions largely within the confines of a unique domestic culture and cannot correctly be understood without reference to that context. Everything from attitudes toward and perceptions of philanthropy, as reflected in governing laws, to the apparatus for raising funds and awarding grants reflects traces of Japanese history and culture. History is continually progressing and culture perpetually evolving; accordingly, philanthropy cannot remain static. Japanese philanthropy is not likely to metamorphose dramatically to reappear suddenly in altered form. It is not likely ever to duplicate the American model. Nonetheless, it has grown and continues to grow into an increasingly sophisticated and effective shape of its own. The final pages of this book briefly examine recent trends and potential future directions in Japanese corporate philanthropy.

As we mentioned earlier, Japanese corporate philanthropy is largely a product of the 1960s. During this period, the growth of corporate international philanthropy was perhaps the most rapid. It is estimated that Japanese donors have contributed over ¥29 billion ($200 million) to foreign organizations since 1975.[1] Moreover, according to a survey by the JCIE in 1985, the rate of growth of direct corporate contributions for international purposes (i.e., contributions not made through separately established corporate foundations) has far exceeded the rate of growth for domestic contributions. In addition to direct corporate contributions, Japanese corporate foundations contribute over ¥2 billion per year to international programs.[2] Of these internationally minded foundations, more than 70 percent have been established since the late 1960s, and at least twelve with assets exceeding ¥1 billion each have been established since 1987.

Thus far, the bulk of Japan's international corporate philanthropy has been targeted to the United States. This trend was probably begun by the Japan Foundation, which was established in 1972 largely in response to U.S. reminders that the cultural exchange between Japan and the United States was relying primarily on American funding. The initiation of the Japan Foundation's programs was quickly followed by a succession of news-generating, blockbuster grants to U.S. universities, museums, and large research institutions.

The priority placed on the United States is reflected in the Japan Foundation's documentation of "designated donations" made by private companies to overseas organizations with Japan Foundation assistance. Although the percentage of such contributions going to the United States has declined over the past several years, the dollar amount has not, and the United States still receives a dominant share.[3]

According to Mr. Tadashi Yamamoto, there are several reasons why the United States has been given such a major portion of Japanese philanthropic funds:

> First of all, it is a reflection of the paramount importance Japanese people attach to the U.S.–Japan relationship. Related is the obvious interest Japanese business holds in cultivating strong links with its most vital trading partner. When trade tensions are aggravated, an emphasis is placed on making grants to American institutions because of their subsequent public relations dividends. Another somewhat related factor is the sense of indebtedness that some Japanese business leaders feel for past American generosities, dating to the postwar reconstruction period.[4]

Perhaps the most significant recent trend in Japanese international philanthropy has been the rise of Japanese-funded private foundations set up in the United States and elsewhere. The first of these U.S.-based corporate foundations was the U.S.–Japan Foundation, established by the Japan Shipbuilding Industry Foundation in 1980 with an endowment of $70 billion, followed in 1985 by the Matsushita Foundation (Matsushita Electric Corporation of America) with an endowment of $10 million and the Hitachi Foundation (Hitachi America, Ltd.) with an endowment of $20 million.[5] The shift to this type of corporate philanthropy is linked to the enormous increase in Japanese overseas direct investment and, in particular, to direct investment in the United States since 1980. Like U.S. domestic corporations, Japanese corporations doing business in the United States have had to learn to be good corporate citizens. The establishment of such overseas foundations is an especially hopeful sign, because they are themselves an experiment in intercultural cooperation and hence one of the most effective types of international philanthropy. More importantly, the creation of corporate foundations signals a deeper, longer-term commitment to local causes and projects than that represented by the large, flashy direct corporate grants. In the past few years, many of these large, corporate grants, and the quid pro quo expected in return for them, have sparked resentment and led to charges of unseemly influence buying by Japanese companies in the United States.[6]

It is expected that Japanese corporate foundations in the United States will continue to multiply, paralleling Japan's expanded business investment. In addition, there are signs that even direct corporate giving is on the verge of becoming more responsive and responsible. As we mentioned in the preceding chapter, in 1988 the Keidanren established an affiliate organization in the United States — the Council for Better Investment in the U.S.A. — part of whose function is to advise companies on appropriate means of contributing to their local business communities. In order to encourage this type of activity, the Ministry of International Trade and Industry and the Ministry of Finance have approved a plan to allow corporate headquarters in Japan to make tax-deductible contributions directly to U.S. nonprofit organizations, provided that such contributions are funneled through the Council for Better Investment or similar organizations. It is not yet clear exactly how this plan will be implemented, but the arrangement is intended to be similar to the Japan Foundation's middleman mechanism, except that the range of allowable contributions will not be limited to those contributing to the dissemination of Japanese culture.

Recently, pressures for Japan to internationalize have been particularly strong with respect to Japan's relationship to the rest of Asia. This has been reflected in the government's focus on increasing and improving the quality of Japan's official development assistance (ODA)—including proposals to increase assistance to nongovern-mental organizations (NGOs)—as well as in debates about expand-ing Japan's role in the Asian Development Bank. Corporate philan-thropists are also beginning to respond, albeit slowly, to such pressure. Designated donations to various Asian countries made through the Japan Foundation reached approximately $7 million in 1985, and approximately 41 percent ($39 million) of the Japan Foundation's own program expenditures were devoted to Asia and Oceania.[7]

Since its founding in 1975, the Toyota Foundation has dedicated the major part of its international activity to making grants for the preservation of native cultures throughout Asia. In addition, Toyota has a separate foundation, the Toyota Astra Foundation, in Indonesia. Although the total amounts contributed by most Japa-nese corporations and corporate foundations in Asia remain rela-tively small, the potential for growth is good, as this trend too appears to be linked to increased business investment, particularly in Southeast Asia. Thus, Asahi Glass, a huge petrochemical corpo-ration that is heavily invested in Indonesia and Thailand, contrib-utes to scientific development in those countries through the grant-making activities of the Yaysan Asahi Glass Indonesia Foundation and the Asahi Glass Foundation of Thailand. The Tokyu Corpora-tion, which is heavily invested throughout Asia, supports Asian students studying in Japan through the Tokyu Foundation for In-bound Students.

Despite the rapid internationalization of Japanese corporate phi-lanthropy and the optimism about continued growth in that direc-tion, a few words of caution should perhaps be inserted. First, one of the main reasons for growth in the international realm has been the lack of well-established government policies and institutions to cope with the host of political and economic issues that Japan's international economic expansion has engendered. It is possible that as the government begins to catch up, it will attempt to assert more control over some of these private initiatives. This fear sur-faced recently in the NGO community with the announcement by the Japanese government of a plan to grant subsidies to NGOs as part of its ¥755.7 billion ODA package for fiscal 1989. Although the total subsidy amount available is quite small—¥112 million—it has sparked debate among NGO organizations as to whether accepting such funds will lead to untoward government intervention in these largely private, largely voluntary activities.

Second, "internationalization," although an extremely popular buzzword, has in fact been confined to a relatively small circle in Japan. There is not much doubt that internationalization will continue, but the rate at which it will progress and the depth to which it will penetrate are subject to some question. Speaking at a 1986 symposium at the International House of Japan, Kazuo Nukuzawa, director of the International Economic Affairs Department of the Keidanren, stated: "I don't think Japanese on the whole are pleased with the idea of progressing with internationalization."[8] Business, of course, has been the primary catalyst for internationalization in both the for-profit and the nonprofit realms, and it is likely to continue to be so. Nonetheless, the development of a more well rounded, more effective international philanthropy will ultimately depend on a broader base of support for internationalization.[9]

What then of domestic philanthropy? Like international grant making, domestic corporate philanthropy in Japan is largely a contemporary phenomenon. Over 75 percent of the private nonprofit organizations in Japan today have been formed since 1965.[10] Despite the dramatic growth in the numbers of organizations, the entities themselves are still relatively small and unknown, and their expansion is slow, "rather like water dripping and seeping slowly into the desert," according to Mr. Seiichi Mitani of the Mitsubishi Bank Foundation.[11]

As I discussed in Chapter 2, a variety of cultural and historical factors have combined to inhibit the growth of domestic philanthropy in Japan on a scale comparable to that in the United States. In considering the future of domestic philanthropy, then, we shall first look at the rationales advanced for U.S. philanthropy and ask whether such a system, or any part of it, really makes sense inside Japan.

In the United States, private foundations are seen as an essential and integral part of a democratic, pluralistic society to which they contribute "moral qualities of decency and humanity. Like the entire private nonprofit sector . . . foundations offer a means of expression for the sense of individual responsibility to serve the needs of others."[12] In addition, it is believed that private philanthropy accomplishes socially necessary and desirable work that otherwise would be done by the government but can be done with "more

imagination, diversity, flexibility or economy" by private organizations.[13] In this regard, the existence of a vigorous private sector is an
affirmation of the principle of limited rather than unlimited government and, in the view of Waldemar Nielson, acts as a check against
the deadening effects of excessive official bureaucracy and regula-
tion.[14]

Measured against these postulates, it would seem that the case
for such private initiatives in Japan is weak. Japan is homogeneous, not diverse and pluralistic; individual action is discouraged,
not venerated; and centralized government and powerful bureaucracy are welcomed, not feared. On the other hand, these long-
perpetuated generalizations are beginning to show signs of wear.
Although not racially pluralistic, Japan is in other ways becoming
increasingly diverse. Discrepancies in wealth, education, and exposure to the West and other parts of Asia are making themselves felt,
and traditional values, social, and political structures are bending
with the impact.

As we observed earlier, one of the chief determinants of the
generosity of individual donors in the United States is their perception of their own wealth and available, disposable income. Although Japanese have steadfastly adhered to the view that they are
not wealthy as individuals, their greater buying power and increased
number of opportunities to wield that power through international
travel should ultimately alter that view, perhaps providing the necessary impetus to individual philanthropic initiatives. Furthermore,
recent widespread disillusionment with politicians and the en-
trenched political system as the result of widespread stock scandals
have raised, and should continue to raise questions about the role
of government versus the role of individuals in Japanese society.

Moreover, some of the other rationales advanced in support of
private philanthropy in the United States appear to be particularly
applicable to Japan as it makes the transition from an isolated
island country to a major world power. As enumerated by Waldemar Nielson, the functions of private initiatives include

1. the offering of criticism, new policy options, and new and tested
   ideas for the redirection of policies and the improvement of all
   kinds of educational, scientific, cultural and social programs;
2. a softening of the harsh edges and sometimes cruel consequences
   of unrestrained market forces;

3. the provision of an essential adaptive and self-renewing mechanism, a survival mechanism for the societies in which they are allowed to operate . . . in which continuously changing circumstances require the modification of national policies, programs, and institutions.[15]

In the past, according to Ms. Yoshiko Wakayama, director of international programs at the Toyota Foundation, it has been difficult for Japanese to identify areas of domestic need to which philanthropic enterprises might contribute; pinpointing such areas of concern outside Japan has been easier. For example, Ms. Wakayama described the visit of a large Dutch foundation to Japan several years ago: "They came to Japan with the intention of funding some kind of program here and had a particular interest in supporting projects for troubled children. This is something they try to do in all countries with which the founding corporation has an important business relationship. After touring Japan, the foundation representative was unsure where and if there was a need in Japan for any such program. He finally decided to give aid to children of single parents, but it was difficult to identify a cause."[16]

Although this may have been a problem in the past, certainly today Japan has need of "new policy options," a "softening of the harsh edges" of market forces, and "an adaptive and self-renewing mechanism" as it grapples with domestic problems and newfound prosperity. With the most rapidly aging population in the world, increasing disparities in wealth accumulation and distribution, dramatically soaring land costs, and job displacement resulting from *endaka* (the high value of the yen) and the gradual eclipse of heavy industry by high-tech industries—to name just a few—the opportunities for private philanthropy to shape and advance social policy and to alleviate social problems are rife, albeit still to a large degree unrecognized. Although it would be both impossible and undesirable for Japanese philanthropy to duplicate U.S.-style philanthropy, there is unquestionably a role for a strong third sector in Japan. To date, however, that role has been underplayed.

Notes

1. These figures come from the Japan Foundation's statistics on specified donations that have been channeled by the Japan Foundation to foreign organizations. I have assumed, because utilization of the Japan Foun-

130   JAPANESE CORPORATE PHILANTHROPY

dation mechanism has been the only way to receive tax deductions for international contributions, that this represents most of the significant overseas giving. See Japan Foundation, *Outline Annual Report for 1987* (Tokyo: Japan Foundation, 1988), p. 53.

2. Japanese Philanthropy and International Cooperation, *The Role of Philanthropy in International Cooperation*, Report on the JCIE 15th Anniversary, International Symposium (Tokyo: Japan Center for International Exchange, 1985), p. 12 and tables 1–3, pp. 26–28.

The term *international programs* as used in the JCIE study includes the programs of domestic organizations that are involved in "international" activities. Mr. Michio Itō, executive director of JANIC and an associate of JCIE, pointed out that of the almost ¥3 billion contributed by Japanese foundations to "international" causes in 1987, ¥1.78 billion was actually given to Japanese recipients in the form of scholarships or grants for study overseas, support for international academic conferences in Japan, and the like. See Yamamoto and Amenomori, "Japanese Philanthropy in an Interdependent World."

3. Information from the Planning and Accounting Departments, Japan Foundation. The actual category is for North America, but virtually all of these funds have gone to the United States.

4. Japanese Philanthropy and International Cooperation, *The Role of Philanthropy*, p. 17.

5. Other Japanese foundations in the United States include the American Honda Foundation, American Suzuki Motor Foundation, Subaru of America Foundation, Toyota USA Foundation, Ise Cultural Foundation, Optech USA D.D. Fund, Nakamichi Foundation, and Sony Foundation.

6. See William J. Holstein and Amy Borrus, "Japan's Clout in the U.S." (cover story), *Business Week*, July 11, 1988, pp. 30–41. Note especially Leslie Helm, Alice Z. Cuneo, and Dean Foust, "On the Campus: Fat Endowments and Growing Clout," pp. 37–38.

7. Japan Foundation, *Annual Report for 1987*. In 1988, designated contributions made through the Japan Foundation totalled ¥5 billion ($35 million). The Japan Foundation was unwilling to supply a geographic breakdown of this number, or of the numbers for any years after 1985.

8. Kazue Nukuzawa speaking at "The Internationalization of Japanese Business," symposium at the International House of Japan, November 11, 1986.

9. One of the most encouraging recent developments in this regard was the formation in 1988 of the Japan NGO Center for International Cooperation (JANIC), under the leadership of Mr. Michio Itō. This organization is intended to provide support, expertise, and information to the approximately 270 NGOs currently active in Japan, approximately 33 percent of

which have been formed by private citizens' groups with no corporate or government affiliation.

10. *Nihon no josei-gata zaidan yōran — 1985 nemban* (Directory of Japan's grant-making foundations — 1985 edition) compiled by the Japan Center for International Exchange, the Japan Association of Charitable Corporations, and the Toyota Foundation.

11. Interview with Mr. Seiichi Mitani, September 26, 1986.

12. Nielson, "The Roles of Private Grant-making Foundations," p. 35.

13. Bittker, "Charitable Contributions," pp. 37 and 39.

14. Nielson, "The Roles of Private Grant-making Foundations," p. 36.

15. Ibid., pp. 34–37.

16. Interview with Ms. Yoshiko Wakayama, director of international programs, Toyota Foundation, July 29, 1986.

Index